The End of Therapy

Why Talk Therapy Is In Decline,
And What You Can Do About It

by Sharon Small

The End of Therapy

Why Talk Therapy Is In Decline, And What You Can Do About It

"The End of Therapy" investigates why psychotherapy is in decline and attempts to identify what contributing factors may be present within our most common talk therapy practices. It then explores the impact of those factors on clients and consequently on the therapy sector as a whole, and finally sets out a vision for a healthier model for the 21st Century, which practitioners can start to integrate immediately with the methods and models that they are currently using.

This book is not intended to be a comprehensive study, but a bird's eye view of some macro-patterns that are being used in the most common therapeutic models in use today – along with some common beliefs within that sector.

The new model of working with clients that the book introduces is just a taste of what can be accomplished with the latest methods, the most salient pieces being touched on only lightly while addressing the six most endemic macro-patterns in use today.

Over the past decades the field of cognitive science, cognitive linguistics and self-organizing systems has come a long way, but it has yet to interface with the historical philosophy and theory of psychology and thinking of the general public. And yet, it is evident when researching these fields that the knowledge and understanding of how we make meaning is in metaphor, analogy and simile. In other words, we mean what we say and say what we mean – even if its meaning is clear only to ourselves.

Psychology is just now beginning to catch up with some of the deep insights from the previously mentioned fields through developments such as Clean Language, Symbolic Modeling,

Focusing, Generative NLP and other methods drawing on some of the insights and information contained in them.

Written in an easy to read and informative style, this is a highly accessible guide to understanding some of the larger patterns being used in the therapy rooms of today and how we might approach the mental health and care of our clients more effectively, and hopefully re-establish psychotherapy's position as the most trusted treatment solution in the West.

Copyright Information

The End Of Therapy: Why Talk Therapy Is In Decline, and What You Can Do About It

by Sharon Small Copyright © 2015

Printed in the United States Of America.

First Printing, 2015

ISBN-13: 9781508886815

ISBN-10: 1508886814

Little Books Press / Clean Language Institute
Po Box 351
Arroyo Grande, CA 93420

www.littebookspress.com

Thank you for respecting the hard work of this author.

Table of Contents

Introduction

It is an indisputable fact that psychotherapy is currently in a long period of gradual decline in the United States.

In the early 1990s, over 71% people of people with depression said their treatment included therapy. By 1997, that number had dropped to just 60%.[1]

Today, over half of patients receive no therapy at all and rely on medication alone.[2] Why should that be?

According to this 2005 article by the American Association of Family Physicians, there is no compelling evidence to say that either antidepressants or any particular model of psychotherapy or talk therapy has any particular advantage in the treatment of depression (which is predicted to be the second most common cause of disability worldwide):

> For adults with mild to moderate depression, there is no direct evidence that drug or non-drug therapy is superior. Prescription antidepressants are effective at all levels of severity, but systematic reviews have shown no differences in outcomes between any classes of antidepressants. Different types of psychotherapy (including cognitive therapy and interpersonal psychotherapy) are also effective for managing mild to moderate depression. However, consistent evidence is lacking to make a statement about the relative effectiveness of different types of psychotherapies compared with each other or with drug treatment.[3]

Some of the reasons for the decline are purely economic. In the United States, private medical insurance will frequently pay for antidepressants, whereas more costly therapy may get only limited funding.

Another major factor must be the innovation in the development (and the marketing) of antidepressants such as Prozac®. Drug manufacturers invest such large sums of capital for research and development, it becomes critical that they take market share. They have naturally adopted a more aggressive approach to marketing the relative benefits of their products.

In 2004, the psychotherapy industry in the United States was worth almost $9 billion.[4] By contrast, in the same year the pharmaceutical industry was worth around $235 billion, making it *twenty-five times bigger*.

Therapy is facing a far better-resourced and better-organized competitor. But the therapy sector, as the incumbent solution provider, does not perceive any real sense of urgency. While therapy's success rates are generally shown to be comparable to pharmaceutical treatments, there seems to be little motivation within the profession to publicize the fact.

Maybe therapy is losing the public relations battle. That is not made easier for individual therapists by the ethical problems of promoting their services to a customer base that is by nature vulnerable. The American Psychological Association's own ethical principles include the following guidance:

> [5.06] Psychologists do not engage, directly or through agents, in uninvited in-person solicitation of business from actual or potential therapy clients/patients or other persons who because of their particular circumstances are vulnerable to undue influence.

Regulations vary from state to state. Soliciting or accepting pay for referrals is absolutely illegal in California, while other states have no regulation at all, though it is generally viewed as unethical to request or to solicit testimonials from psychotherapy clients, or to use clients' personal testimony in promotional materials.

Of course there are several good reasons for this. First, it might create an unreasonable expectation that similar results could be guaranteed for other clients, which would be inappropriate in any clinical context. Second are the obvious confidentiality issues. Third, the relationship between client and therapist is integral to the client's treatment and to use that relationship for self-promotion would create a conflict of interest.

It is interesting to note that coaching, although it may share many of the same methods and goals of therapy, is bound by none of these constraints, and that may be one factor contributing to the current exodus of therapists into the coaching sector.

These constraints generally apply to the individual practising therapist, leaving little incentive for them to collect data on successes. But they do not account for the lack of a coordinated campaign to keep the efficacy of therapy in general at the forefront of the American consciousness.

We should acknowledge that the marketing of pharmaceutical treatments is not subject to the same kinds of restrictions, getting into our homes and attention through magazine articles and TV commercials. These promote prescription medications, not over the counter, with subtle cues to self-diagnose and request a prescription from your doctor... "Ask your doctor if _____ is right for you?".

Now that it has a greater choice in cheaper and comparably effective alternatives, is the American public losing its faith in the ability of psychotherapy to deliver results? Is therapy becoming unfashionable, perhaps seen as just another modern habit, an on-going series of expensive consultations with no real purpose, *and no end*?

Considering that therapy may incur significant costs in time and money, and does not promise a timely positive conclusion, it should not be surprising that therapy may start to appear less appealing than antidepressants.

It is time for the therapy sector to take its head out of the sand and to get a voice. While the profession certainly enjoyed boom years in previous decades, with a seemingly evergreen customer base, we simply cannot take that for granted in years to come.

So what can therapy do to save itself?

First, it would seem there is a need for the profession to do a better job of organizing its resources to remind the public about the effectiveness of talk therapy and its compelling benefits relative to drug treatment.

But there is a second, possibly even more difficult, challenge that the profession faces today: that is to bring itself into the twenty-first century and to get into better shape. Can we take it for granted that techniques developed decades ago are still fit for purpose today?

If we accept that therapy alone is not categorically more effective than drug treatments, *could it be*?

Are there handicaps that today's most popular talk therapy models inherit, which may inhibit their potential to deliver clear and lasting results?

If so, what are they, and what can therapists do to transform the valuable service they provide in a way that improves its results and assures its place in the future of the American healthcare system?

Perhaps it is time to close one chapter on psychotherapy, and to begin a new one.

I wrote this book first to explore, honestly and frankly, what those constraining factors may be. Then I want to ask what a shift to a better way might require, and to start to imagine a brighter future for therapy: one that can inspire therapists to move forward with renewed confidence and inspiration.

About The Author

Although I am not a practising licensed psychotherapist, I have extensive experience, both on the practice side, working with many clients in a therapeutic context, and as a therapy client.

In practice, I have worked extensively with NLP, hypnosis, and various personality typologies (such as MBTI and Ennea-gram), as well as interdenominational spiritual direction.

I have trained many therapists in complementary methods. However, I have found most of those methods to be ultimately unsatisfying and unrewarding.

I have also had plenty of experience of therapy on the client side. Our family history had our whole family attending early group therapy in the 1970's. I also experienced sexual abuse as a child and later physical abuse as an adult. As a result, over many years I experienced a range of therapy models, from transactional analysis, talk therapy (in the model of Virginia Satyr), to Jungian archetypal work.

I found that the therapeutic models framed me as either a victim or a survivor and I did not find that either role hon-ored me or my ultimate goal of living as a whole, healthy human being. I was often given advice or unwanted pity, and was treated as though I was broken, weak, or inherently wrong. I even started to become an expert in my *wrongness*. But none of these tools or techniques delivered the changes I craved.

I began to notice a common thread. Both as a client, and then later in practice, there was a reason so many therapeutic techniques did not feel right for me. That is because they all used some framework that is essentially manipulative, based on an assumption that *the therapist knows better than the client about what the client needs.*

When I started to pull on that thread, the fundamental model of psychotherapy started to unravel, with surprising results.

Why Therapy Isn't Working

Every therapist I have met went into practice for the same reason: to help people. With the foundation of that sincere desire we also apply what we've been taught, and what we've learned over the years through experience, to try to help our clients to feel happy, positive, and free, so they can go on to enjoy healthy lives.

If we're honest, though, it doesn't always work out that way. How many clients *really* get the lasting results we know are possible? Across the sector, clearly positive results are typically achieved 40%-60% of the time.[6]

In recent years, I have noticed a trend where significant numbers of therapists are moving into being certified as coaches. Is that because demand for therapy is starting to dry up? Or could it be that what they are doing in therapy is simply not delivering a steady stream of successful cases, so they are looking for alternative structured methods? I believe the latter is true: that *in general*, therapy is not working.

I do not wish to suggest that *all* therapy is unhelpful. On the contrary! I have seen many people benefit greatly from therapy, and I know some who would probably not be alive today if it was not for having timely access to good therapists.

I also have enormous respect for anyone who devotes their professional life to helping others in this way. It is a difficult and challenging area, probably one which often seems we're only starting to understand, so I see today's therapists among the pioneers. If you are a practising therapist today, you have my undying admiration. I want you to know I deeply honor the work you do, and the motivation that brought you into this discipline.

I wrote this book *precisely because* I have so much respect for this profession, for all its practitioners, and for their clients. The work that therapists do is vital to individuals, to families, and to communities, we all bear a massive responsibility to ensure we are delivering the very best service we can.

We know that therapy can work, but we also know that its is not always successful. And, as we've seen, there is now a growing pharmaceutical industry investing massive resources to promote its new, alternative biological treatments, so the therapy sector either needs to start to compete better, or face a slow decline.

If we truly believe in the work we do, we cannot rest on our laurels, trusting that everyone who needs our help will automatically know that our methods are better, safer, and longer-lasting than drug treatments. After all, many of the most fundamental therapeutic techniques in use today were developed in the last century.

If therapy is going to compete, I think we must apply the scientific method. That means we should never assume that the techniques and models we were taught are the final solution, and we must always be open to opportunities to welcome new insights and to use them to improve the way we work. We should continue to draw on not only the best from neuroscience, but also the recent significant advances in cognitive linguistics, cognitive science, and self-organizing systems theory.

I invite you to consider a challenging question. What if the general failure of talk therapy is a result of shortcomings that are built into *fundamental model of talk therapy itself*?

In the following chapters, I will identify what I believe are a number of common weaknesses in the very foundation of the model of psychotherapy. I will show how those weaknesses are inherited by practically every talk therapy method in use today. In the cases when therapy works, it works *in spite* of these weaknesses.

Next I'll examine what needs to happen in order to make our

methods more effective.

Finally, we'll start to imagine how much more successful therapy could be if we could deliver it *free from* those endemic shortcomings, and conclude with a vision for what a model for therapy in the 21st century could look like, and how that could play a major part in the future of *your* practice.

Let's start by asking, when therapy fails, why does it fail?

Where Is The Fault?

A common frustration among therapists is seeing the same clients for months (or even years) without seeing any real change in the client's thinking or behavior. That raises serious questions. How does a therapist begin to address the problem of a stubborn lack of results?

There are logically only three areas we can point to: our clients; our abilities; or our methods. Let's look at each of these in turn.

Is the Client at Fault?

It is not uncommon for therapists to lay the responsibility for the failure of therapy with the client. For example, an article at PsychCentral title "10 Reasons Why Therapy May Not Be Working"[7] cited five questions therapists should ask themselves when therapy is failing, which it follows with five plausible reasons why *the patient may be responsible*.

It certainly seems apparent that one of the scenarios that more therapists report is what we call "resistant clients." That is, clients whom we judge as uncooperative, or who do not deliver on their commitments. But can a professional honestly stand by the claim that, if their service has a low success rate, it is usually down to a failure on the part of the client?

There's an old joke in psychotherapy circles...

> "How many therapists does it take to change a light bulb?"

> "Only one, but the light bulb has got to *want* to change."

I just cannot accept that labeling any individual client as

"resistant" can be a valid excuse for the failure of therapy. Can we truly say that a client who pays fees to a professional, and who shows up to sessions for months or even years is not interested in, or committed to, change? I don't think we can do that with integrity.

And even if it is true that some clients are resistant to the process, what causes that resistance? If what the therapist is doing is not working for the client, is it appropriate to insist that *the client change* to suit the therapy? Is it unreasonable to expect the therapy to suit the client?

Is the Therapist at Fault?

For similar reasons, we cannot lay the blame at the therapist's feet either.

Practically all the therapists I have ever known are highly educated, highly trained, highly professional, have their clients' best interests at heart, and are committed to seeing conclusive successful outcomes for those clients.

I believe that factor alone means we cannot logically argue that failure of therapy is the fault of the individual therapist. Surely any ineffective therapists would be weeded out of practice, either by lack of fulfilment, or through economics.

One 2012 research project explored the relative impact of the various factors that can influence successful therapy, and concluded...

> The therapeutic alliance remains a key component of creating successful outcomes in psychotherapy. Empathy also continues to be an integral factor to not only forming the alliance, but also increasing a client's ability to feel validated and understood. It appears that experience does not always increase the odds of creating successful outcomes in therapy, and no one type of therapeutic modality is superior to another. The findings also concur that a client's level of motiva-

tion, personality characteristics, and symptomatology do play a role in their therapeutic outcomes.[8]

We might speculate that it comes down to personalities. Maybe some clients just don't suit some therapists, or vice versa. There is probably some truth to the idea that the specific combination of personalities is one contributing factor among many, but could it play such a major role? And could that account for the general failure rate across the whole spectrum? To suggest this would be to admit that none of our therapeutic methods is robust enough to deliver repeated results irrespective of personality clashes.

If creating the "therapeutic alliance" is a critical prerequisite to successful therapy, any therapist who was less able to do that would also struggle to provide a competitive service, and we would see far more distinctive differences in performance levels between practitioners.

Because I have found no evidence to indicate that the general failure of therapy can be attributed to a variation in performance between individual practitioners, I think it stands to reason that it cannot be down to the therapists.

Is the Method at Fault?

That just leaves us with the method. If it isn't the client, and it isn't the therapist, it has to be the therapeutic model that isn't working. And I believe that to be the case.

The "Dodo Bird Verdict" is an idea that attempts to explain that the reason all models of talk therapy seem, suspiciously, to work broadly as well as each other must be down to factors that are common to all methods.[9]

Let's explore this, and assume it is true that all models are similarly successful.

What's really intriguing to me is not why they are similarly successful. After all, these are methods that have been practised and improved for a long time - they *should* provide benefit, and much of the time they are all effective to some degree. If they provide benefit for common reasons, such as forming a relationship with a kindly expert and having the space to talk openly and to be listened to without criticism, we might ask why talk therapy isn't helpful *more of the time.*

What I think is really surprising is that all methods appear to *fail at a similar rate*!

Because there are no clear differences in the measurable effectiveness of the various models of psychotherapy, we can infer that if there are problems with therapy, their root causes must be *present in all current practices.* If it is not that one school or approach is bringing down the overall average, the problem must be with *talk therapy itself.*

I must acknowledge that the concept that therapy isn't working may be a challenging idea to entertain. It requires an investment of thousands of dollars and around three thousand client hours to become a licensed psychotherapist in the US today. If you have been on that journey, you will have a lot invested in therapy *working*!

Furthermore, whatever our particular field, we all received our training from learned and respectable people. To consider challenging our shared belief and faith in these methods could feel like a betrayal of our mentors and educators.

We should also acknowledge that we have a shared cultural belief in this country that *therapy works.* However, the fact that something is generally accepted does not make it true. Although psychotherapy, as we know it, has been practiced for over a century, until very recently no one has undertaken robust studies into its effectiveness.

Taking an open-minded position, we must first accept that therapy is not universally effective. It works for some clients, some of the time.

The question we are faced with, then, is this: Why does talk therapy so consistently succeed for some clients and fail for others?

And then we need to ask, how it might *work better*?

Of course our mind's natural response is to generate reasons to explain away the evidence. However, I would request you try to suspend that kind of instinctive reaction, at least for a short time. It takes courage and integrity to question our deepest-held beliefs. All I ask is that you give me the opportunity to present the reasons why I think therapy is failing.

I will then explore how we can change the way we work to deliver what we all truly want: lasting, positive change for our clients, so that they can move on with their lives after therapy.

Six Factors that May Contribute to the Failure of Therapy

I have identified the following six factors that are common to the popular talk therapy methods in use today, and which I believe may contribute to the failure of therapy for a significant number of clients:

- Unequal power relationship

- Operating in the realm of brokenness

- Intrusive methods

- Goal-less

- Externalizing responsibility

- Dependency

1. Unequal Power Relationship

The very way the therapist-client relationship is set up from the outset creates an obstacle in the way of some clients to achieve true and lasting change.

When one person is in the position of expert, and a client comes to them because they are an expert, that sets up an unequal power relationship that supposes the therapist should have very significant influence on the client. Even with the best intentions, it is practically impossible to undo that power disparity, because it is implicit from the start of the therapist-client relationship.

Human beings are social animals. We live our lives in the context of reference and associations between ourselves and others. As Stanley Milgram's experiments showed in the

1960's, perceived authority can easily result in subjection, whether intentionally or not.

When the client first enters the room, they bring with them the concept that the therapist can help them. In other words, they start with a reference point that is *extrinsic*. The therapist is supposed to be in charge, and it is their job to influence the client positively. The client's role is faithfully to follow the therapist's lead.

We can see the pattern of the unequal power relationship already evident in the language we use. The word "*psychoanalysis*" denotes that the process requires "analysis," which is of course a specialist activity that must therefore be performed by an expert.

The word "thera*pist*" identifies the actor in the transaction. In other words, when therapy happens, one active person is *doing* what they do to another person, the recipient, who is more passive in the relationship.

This conceptual linguistic structure brings its own connotations. The therapist is playing the active role, therefore the goal or any desired outcome would not be possible without their active involvement. Without a therapist, there can be no therapy. We are left with a sense that therapy is in itself the answer. By extension, the client is incomplete and needs something external (therapy) in order possibly to become complete. Whether they achieve their desired outcome or not depends on the external factor. That might say that the client is *externally referenced*.

However we know that, in order for clients to be masters of their own lives, they must develop the sure knowledge that *they* have the power, the choices, and the ultimate responsibility. In other words, become more *internally or intrinsically referenced*.

How can an *external reference* to the expert help their client to become more *internally referenced*, knowing more about themselves and what they want? Surely it is illogical. How can the therapist return the client's power to them? That is one of the fundamental paradoxes we have to deal with.

To see the reality of the unequal power relationship, we only need to look at the laws that are in place to prevent personal relationships between therapists and their clients. Those laws would not be necessary if the massive disparity in power and influence did not exist.

We might draw parallels with a parent-child relationship, which is worrying in itself, particularly if the client is dealing with issues around family. Does someone who is trying to take greater responsibility in their work, family, or personal relationships need to work that out in an environment with a substitute parent figure? And is there another way?

We could also say that psychotherapists are like a modern-day priesthood, ordained with the authority to intercede on behalf of lay people. In his book, "The Modes and Morals of Psychotherapy" (Routledge, 1986), psychologist Perry London acknowledges both the rise of the new priesthood and the awesome responsibility it confers, but can offer no more than an apologistic response.

> Psychotherapists are not well suited to this priesthood, either by training or by disposition. They must accept it even so, for there is no way fully to separate their technical skills and moral inclinations from their clients' need to act upon the world and live in it, with or without the saving grace of eternal and external authority. Since their only moral recourse is personal faith and experience and to the deductions they make from the ever-changing sciences they study, therapists should face this role with fear and trembling and awe at the responsibility historical circumstance has thrust on them and at the damage they can do to their clients and the world in meeting it. But they must not shirk

it by passing moral responsibility to society; its legislation in capricious. Nor can they pass it decently to their guilds, trading collective conviction for individual courage. Least of all can they saddle clients with total responsibility, once having participated in the problem, until they have shared their opinion on its solution.

We might also speculate about parallels between psychotherapy and the first few steps[10] of the AA Twelve Step program...

1. We admitted we were powerless over alcohol — that our lives had become unmanageable.

2. Came to believe that a Power greater than ourselves could restore us to sanity.

3. Made a decision to turn our will and our lives over to the care of God *as we understood Him.*

While that structure has undoubtedly helped millions of addicts to live clean and sober lives, the "power greater than ourselves" in these programs is not meant to be represented by another person, but "God, as we understand him." What concerns me is that psychotherapy inherits a similar fundamental belief model: that clients are powerless over their problems, and that they require something external in order to return to sanity. What's more, that external power is exercised by another human being.

As we've seen, the therapist is ordained with special power, and they are expected to use that power to influence the client. We just hope that any influence is positive. Because we cannot say with confidence that any therapist is free of prejudices, misconceptions, or blind spots in their own thinking, it is entirely possible that the therapist may be as limited as the client in some crucial aspect.

I must stress that any lack of influence, or negative influence, that therapists have on clients is likely to be unintentional.

The therapists I know share a common, heartfelt intention not to push or to manipulate their clients. What they don't know is that manipulation simply comes with the territory, a direct result of the way the game is set up.

That can lead to a potentially addictive or co-dependent relationship between client and therapist, and what has been coined *transference*. Transference is where a client lays their perceptions and expectations on the therapist, which is a natural result of having an external reference. (The craziest thing about transference and *counter-transference* is that some therapeutic models believe that this is *necessary* for the client to get better and if it isn't happening something is wrong, usually with the client!)

The coaching sector is subject to some of the same issues. Coaches also position themselves as authorities. Clients also approach coaches to get clear on what to do next to get the results they want in their lives. And the solution starts with the external expert, with the coach and their models or processes. Coaches are less likely to delve as deeply and to explore issues that may expose the client, and they are also far less constrained by ethical guidelines.

Particularly when we think about coaches, it's likely there is ego at play. The extreme form of coaching we get from motivational speakers delivers an intense dose of somebody else's powerful ego and ideas, which can be stimulating, and ultimately still an external reference that is unlikely to result in lasting internal change.

It takes a great deal of discipline for a person who holds so much power to take full responsibility for the influence they have on another person. Even with the best intentions, it is impossible to know for sure the outcome of every intervention.

An article from the Zur Institute describes one of the more extreme scenarios...

"Working with people who often idealize you and often are desperate for help and guidance can result in what Ernest Jones labeled 'God Syndrome.' Those who develop such an inflated sense of self are likely to be sarcastic, disconnected, and un-empathetic with clients."[11]

The unequal power relationship is a factor that we can recognize is intrinsic to the therapy environment, and it confers a huge responsibility on the part of the therapist.

In this scenario, how does a client own the power to end therapy? If the therapist has to tell their client that they, the client, hold the power, do they really?

Perhaps the unequal power relationship might account for some failures in all formats of talk therapy. *It is conceivable that a certain proportion of clients are unable to deal with the paradox of having to own their authority in a situation that by default strips them of that authority. As a consequence, that factor alone may account for some of the failure for a certain percentage of clients across the spectrum of talk therapy models.*

We must then ask, is it *necessary* to hold that degree of influence? It would seem that the obvious answer is "Yes, absolutely," for self-evident reasons. That is how the vast majority of therapy is configured.

But is it possible to visualize a relationship without such an unequal power structure? How might we facilitate a client's healing and discovery as adults, without one being in control, without being *the* expert, and without being expected to come up with clever and useful answers?

2. Operating in the Realm of Brokenness

The second factor that I see common to most talk therapies is that they operate in a language of damage, hurt, abuse, and victimhood. Present-day problems are directly associated with past hurts. (You are experiencing this today *because* of those past experiences.)

Perhaps operating in this mode of *past-cause-present-effect* can introduce its own problems. Perhaps that does not suit some clients, and may contribute to the failure of therapy.

I can say with confidence, it did not serve me.

When I was twenty-four, while working in a drama class I had a spontaneous memory about some early experiences of sexual molestation.

It took me about ten years working in the traditional therapy environment to become free. But I did not become free by resolving the past hurt. It took me ten years to really get how sick that environment was! The reason I know it was sick was because everything they were doing and saying to me pointed out how sick I was, and that this experience was influencing my entire life.

In other words, the model required that I play the role of victim of incest. It took years to realize that I would not find happiness within the boundaries that role allowed. I remember almost a jostling in the group sessions to see who was the biggest victim: was it the one who was penetrated, or the one who was viewed?

And, critically, the process seemed to have *no end*. When do you stop being a victim? How long do you have to be a victim? Can you ever get better? And then, when you stop being a victim, you get to be a "survivor" – and then what happens?

I found there was no release in my labeling myself as a victim, a survivor, or anything else. What was I supposed to do with that label? How would it help me in life? It took me years to realize that it could not. I lived in that prison for about ten years. One of the main reasons I kept pursuing therapy was because I had been told that these parts of my life I was finding difficult were *caused by* that event in my past. And for a long time, that's what I believed.

The work I was doing seemed to be founded on two core agreements. One was that therapy is *supposed to work*. The second was the absolute conviction of the therapists that my present experiences were a *direct result of* my past experience, and if I sorted them out (understood them), I'd be OK.

That truism eventually broke down. In college, I liked to go out dancing and party a bit and I had a series of sexual relationships. In the group therapy sessions it was explained to me that not only was my sexual behavior problematic, but also that it was a reaction to my early experience (of being inappropriately touched by someone I trusted).

The reality was that my behavior was not a problem to me. It only became a "problem" when put into a psychological health context, framed by a professional as something undesirable.

However, I was also meeting with women who, we were told, were introverted and frigid as a result of their similar experiences of incest. If it was true that past experiences *directly caused* present difficulties, how could the same cause have such opposite effects?

It was around that time that I finally acknowledged, "This isn't healthy! This is not working for me. I could be stuck doing this for the next sixty years." I stopped working in the model of brokenness. I stopped putting myself in the hands of professionals who knew better. That is when I really got that there was nothing wrong with me. I wasn't sick, and I was not a survivor.

I'm not saying do the professional therapists who tried to help me were doing their work badly, or that they lacked integrity. I am saying they were locked into a *model* of hurt and victimhood. When I stepped into the room, complete with my past traumatic experience, I had to fit into that model. That meant being the victim. But it just did not work for me, because it left no room for resolution or ultimate freedom.

I have one therapist I am working with who is absolutely convinced that *everybody* carries some deep, dark psychological trauma. In working with her I can guarantee that she will drive to find that pain with every client she sees. If the client doesn't present it when they first meet, they will work until they find one, if they want to work with her. Because her model of psychotherapy operates exclusively in the realm of brokenness, it cannot work without its raw material.

If a therapist tells you, for example, "Well, clearly you are that way because you're an adult child of an alcoholic," then whatever else happens in your life you will continue to be defined and limited by what that means. Twenty years later you will still be an adult child of an alcoholic, but you will also be bound to the therapist's definition — as long as you are still dwelling in that agreement.

Because we know repetition reinforces neural pathways, the more you repeat that kind of cause-and-effect as a fact, the stronger its influence grows. It will become a self-evident truth, *whether or not it is helpful in your life.*

The apparent benefit of this type of explanation is obviously that we get something to point at and say, "That's why." It absolves us of some level of personal responsibility. But, even if the cause-effect *were* true, would it deliver a benefit?

The model seems to tell us that we have to pass through the realm of brokenness, victimhood, and hurt in order to come out the other side into a healthier space. But what else will we find in the realm of brokenness than more brokenness? Or what medical intuitive, Caroline Myss, calls "woundology" – where connection and relationship are built around our wounds rather than strengths and desires.

How is anyone supposed to be able to break out of that cycle and create change, while using the methods that focus so intently on the negative and explain today's problems as natural effects that we suffer *because of* something that happened in the past?

Here's how one long-term therapy client described his personal experience to me...

> I wasn't emotionally well and I had years of going to therapy. I knew my therapist would say things about going back to my childhood and we'd do all the same things we had been doing for years. It had bound me to an ineffectiveness. But because of that my experience was torn. I wasn't happy enough to go on living and wasn't suffering enough to kill myself. Talk therapy doesn't add up for me. Essentially it is about people being at the mercy of what has happened to them.

There is no question that our present experience *can* be affected by our past. But it seems to be commonly accepted that if a client understands the past enough, change will happen. However, does understanding a simplistic cause-and-effect minimize the effect?

I think the idea that understanding leads to choice or to change is based on faulty logic. Even the idea that understanding *is a prerequisite for* change to happen is disputable. How does re-living or re-telling stories of past hurt change the present experience? Does it dissipate its impact or exacerbate it? Perhaps acknowledging the fact that something happened can be a helpful step towards acceptance, but not repeating it dozens of times.

We can say finding solutions by going over past events is unreliable at best, at the very least because we know that *retraumatization* is a real phenomenon. If we suffer today *because of* past suffering, and we clearly we cannot *change the fact* of the past suffering, what can we change? Both therapist and client become trapped in that same pattern.

I believe more psychotherapists are finding that asking

"Why..?" questions does not really lead to creating lasting change. "Why..?" questions lead to seemingly logical "x because y" statements. While this approach may appear to lead to greater *understanding*, and may also reinforce the client's story, it is arguable whether that is either accurate or helpful.

This is something I have experienced myself. For eight years I worked with a Jungian analyst, who was both my therapist and mentor. He was very wise and we had a very good relationship. Although I learned a lot about archetypal symbolism, my dreams, and about the way my mind functions that enhanced my inner life, the work did not create noticeable benefit in my day to day relationships or my business.

I don't know of any evidence that understanding results in change. In fact there may be evidence that suggests otherwise. Just look at the recent relative growth of Cognitive Behavioral Therapy compared to conventional talk therapy. In a similar way to many NLP methods, CBT is concerned with *changing behavior from the outside in*, so it does not take the past as its starting point. Some studies have even suggested that CBT is generally slightly more effective than classic talk therapies. What does this tell us about the common assumption that we need to understand the past in order to effect change in the future?

CBT, developed in the early 1970s, is experiencing a comeback. One factor in its resurgence may be that it is easier to measure results than traditional psychotherapy, as the impact is on behavior, which is extrinsic and observable, compared to internal change that is subjective, relying on first-person reporting.

It reminds me of my mother telling me to "fake it till you make it" (and talking about the science behind smiling and the creation of better moods.) However, you can fake external behavior! But will it make a difference? I am sure on some level it will. And I'm not convinced that observing someone do something differently really means that the person's internal experience has changed.

I only have to look at my own experience to get an insight into this. I have had my own episodes of periodic depression. People who know me would not realize this, because I know how to get up out of bed, brush my teeth, do my hair, put on my clothes, and put on a professional demeanor. I know my internal state was depressed, yet the external activity might satisfy a CBT practitioner.

Despite this, for certain conditions, CBT's methods are comparatively successful to other therapies, disproving the argument that understanding past events is a prerequisite for change.

If understanding did result in healing, if it could help a client to be more whole, gaining a more complete understanding should leave clients feeling confident to end therapy. We only need to look at clients who spend months or years wrestling with the same issues to see that is not the case. People can spend months or years understanding the causal events to ever-deeper levels, but what good does that do? The only explanation for such long-term therapy use must be that understanding, and the idea that it leads to acceptance, is *not enough*.

Knowing why you are imprisoned does not make you any less imprisoned. Understanding that it is because of something that happened in your past is surely more likely to perpetuate the sense of imprisonment if anything. And how could constantly reliving the reasons why you are imprisoned prepare you to walk free?

Perhaps that could also help explain why therapy does not work for some people, in the way it did not work for me.

But do we have to be stuck using a language of damage and coping? What would it be like if we could operate in a different realm, unburdened by these negative concepts, using language that supports and inspires each client? Can we imagine how therapy might work without a victim?

If we're not dealing in the realm of brokenness, we could say that we are operating in the realm of logic and wholism. Everything the client may think and everything they may do has its own unique logic to it, and they are a whole, they are a system. Our position is neutral.

It is perfectly natural for a therapist, in their assumed position as expert, to feel sympathy for the *damaged* client, and to endeavor to fix them. However, the solution the client really needs may not come from the outside. In fact, an external intervention may create more problems.

3. Intrusive Methods

Until the late nineteenth century, any medical surgery carried significant additional associated risks. If patients survived surgery, they had a good chance of developing a different complication that would kill them. The reason, of course, is that people at the time were not aware of the existence of harmful microbes, and they didn't realize that the dirty equipment they were using was directly contributing to patient mortality.

Survival rates increased dramatically after British scientist Joseph Lister spotted the links between lack of cleanliness, infection, and mortality. Lister advocated the use of certain acids in surgical theaters to create a sterile environment, which led to a dramatic improvement in survival rates. Yet even in an evidence-based model such as medicine it took over a generation before Lister's antiseptic models were wholly adopted by the surgical community.

I believe there are parallels with the practice of psychotherapy today.

In surgery, the highly-trained expert uses *intrusive techniques* to enter the patient's anatomy, with the intention of locating and repairing or removing the sick or malfunctioning organ, or removing a foreign body.

If the patient is lucky, the exercise does not pollute any other part of the environment, no malignant foreign organism is introduced, no other organ is damaged in the procedure, and they are sewn up with all the important pieces in place, so that they can carry on with an improved quality of life.

Psychotherapy is strangely similar. Here, the highly-trained expert also uses *intrusive techniques* to delve into the patient's psyche, with the aim of locating and fixing or removing some element that is sick or malfunctioning (such as limiting beliefs or self-destructive thoughts).

If the client is lucky, the exercise does not pollute anything else in their psychic environment, no unhelpful foreign *ideas* are introduced, no healthy *thinking* is corrupted in the procedure, and they are left whole and able to carry on with an enhanced quality of life.

Freud often used surgical metaphors, in which the psychoanalyst is the surgeon and psychoanalysis a carefully wielded scalpel.

It is common to hear the word "intervention" used to describe a therapist's methods. In the article[12] I referred to earlier, one of the questions the author, Elvira G. Aletta, Ph.D., suggests therapists ask when therapy fails is, "Are our interventions accessible to the patient? In other words, are we giving our patient tools within their reach? Tools they can use?"

What I find remarkable about these questions is that it assumes that the client does not already possess the intrinsic capacity to become whole, so it must be introduced from the outside, through some external *introjection*.

I see three serious problems with this approach.

One is that the practice is intrusive or even invasive in nature. Clearly, as in surgery, any intrusive method requires that extreme care be exercised. If you are going to enter into another human being's psyche, can you be one hundred percent sure that you have accounted for all the potential consequences of every action? Is that even possible?

The second problem is that, in the process of trying to clear existing problems, we risk introducing new ones. Nearly every school of therapy uses its own mental models, concepts and structures. When we use these models in an "open surgery" environment, there is a chance that we could replace one problematic thought process with a different problematic thought process, similar to a 19th century surgery patient contracting a secondary infection.

I can share a recent example from my own experience. I recently participated in a workshop with a group of coaches and holistic healers. At one point, one of the women in the group stood up and said, "I came here thinking I was whole and have everything I need. I'm doing the best I can. Now I realize I have *blocks*." But "blocks" was not her language. She did not arrive with "blocks" – they did not exist to her until they were introduced by others. Suddenly, she was not as whole and complete as she had been when she walked into the room that morning.

What concerns me is how naturally most people will buy that kind of story. In fact, there is a whole industry of quasi-religious or personal development "cults" that rely on that very phenomenon. They can very easily present you with a whole catalog of problems you didn't previously know you had.

In the same way that Catholicism has the concept of *original sin*, the various forms of traditional psychotherapy can start from an assumption that everyone has something wrong with them: some deep-seated wound or trauma. Therapy can then become a solution looking for a problem, saying to clients, "You are not whole, you are naturally imperfect, and if you are willing to do the work we will find where you're broken."

I think that is what I experienced as a therapy client in my college years. I brought with me a distressing memory, but the model required a present-day problem to work on, which is why it focused on my sexual activity, while at the same time addressing the sexual paralysis of other women who'd had experiences that were parallel to mine.

That brings us on to the third problem, which derives from to the previous factor we discussed: operating in the realm of brokenness. If we are dealing only with concepts, ideas and language that focus on what is "wrong" with the patient, surely that creates a "dirty" environment.

Classic psychotherapy tends to explain problems of the mind in terms of other problems, which are often historical and therefore impossible to change. How can we expect a person to become healed and whole when we are constrained to using the language of past pain, guilt, fear, and abuse, and focusing on similar negative present consequences?

We already questioned the extent to which understanding may result in change. Most psychotherapy takes real, *embodied* experiences from the client's past and pushes them up into the cerebellum so that they can be dealt with cognitively, in the assumption that doing so will somehow change the psychic experience. (Embodied cognition describes the way we know things to be true, being held in body consciousness through our experiences of the world, and the schemas we develop through those experiences.)

I have heard therapists describe their job as, "to help the client understand what happened to them." Someone could spend years trying to understand why their father hit them. It doesn't change that fact, and it doesn't help them to have the life they want now. How does shifting a memory from a visceral body memory up to a conscious idea in the neocortex make any real difference? In reality, in doing that, we are just creating another idea: something else for the client to think about, to worry about, or to use as an excuse.

I would ask, how effective is it – even how *healthy* is it – to continually drag up and revisit past hurts? Let's agree that some clients benefit by learning to accept that painful events happened. But is it possible that others find that experience detrimental to their mental health and wellbeing?

Perhaps models that operate intrusively with *dirty* concepts only work for some people, some of the time. Perhaps there is a proportion of clients whom it cannot serve, contributing to the failure of therapy.

How can we expect clients to find wholeness in that environment, and so come to a satisfactory conclusion? It took me ten years to realize that I would not find wholeness in therapy that only understood brokenness. I had to make the choice to step out of therapy whose models had me as "broken" because that is all they knew.

We could argue that the very way the environment is set up, with an unequal power relationship, intrusive techniques, and an obsession with the negative, is the ideal environment to *create problems*!

Instead of entering into a client's psyche, and with all its inherent risks, we might consider that perhaps it is possible to help clients more effectively by *remaining outside*, by endeavoring to introduce as little as possible that was foreign to the client, which includes our own models, concepts, and ideas.

If that were possible it would require a huge shift in thinking. We would first need to accept that human beings, far from being naturally broken, actually already possess the resources they need to be whole and complete, just as they are. I'm not saying that life will always be easy, there will always be challenges and difficulties, but that we each have what we need to cope.

4. Goal-less

It is surprisingly common for traditional therapists not to know what the client wants. They may know why they're there... "I'm not getting along with my spouse", "I have this bad memory", "I'm depressed", "I'm struggling", etcetera. A therapist will likely make assumptions from what the client says, inferring what they want, but that does not necessarily tell us what the client actually wants and what the conditions need to be for them to complete the therapy and to move on.

In the context of an unequal power relationship, it must surely be the responsibility of the expert in charge to ensure the boundaries for the engagement are defined. But I have heard first-hand from many therapists that they can have multiple sessions with a new client without the client ever expressing what they want the outcome of their therapy to be. And even when the client does express what they want to happen, it is likely to be translated, deprioritized, or forgotten during the course of the sessions.

We can assume that both therapist and client share a common goal, which is the client's wellbeing. There is a big step from acknowledging that to defining it clearly, which is rarely achieved and frequently not even attempted. If we don't *know what healing means to that client and what they will have as a result*, how can either party know when it has been achieved?

Without any outcome in place, therapy almost seems to have become a popular pastime. That is certainly an easy conclusion to get from popular American culture: therapy seems to be part of everyday life according to many Hollywood movies, celebrities, and comedians.

As we have seen, the universal need for therapy is based on an assumption that each of us is messed up. When we accept that and go into therapy, we can only really expect to uncover and to revisit past traumas. And because we are working in a dirty environment with intrusive methods, we might discover new problems we did not originally know we had, which of course necessitates further therapy!

Therapy therefore can become an end in itself: an activity that can be part of regular life, without any other purpose or end in sight. Is it even reasonable to expect any other outcome?

So who says when the therapy is done? Even if the client were empowered through the therapeutic relationship to make that call, they would first have to know their desired outcome, and then to recognize when that outcome is reached. But if it is assumed that the client is not the expert, and if they do not hold the power, how feasible is that?

For the therapist to end the course of treatment would also require a desired outcome, ideally one that is agreed with the client. But, as we have already seen, if the therapy is based on using intrusive methods that dig past trauma up out of the dirt, how can that ever result in a clean environment on which to conclude?

5. Externalizing Responsibility

As social beings, we naturally look around as at other people in order to determine what we should do or not do. As we have already seen, the external reference — accepting that another person knows better than we do how we should be — is the default starting point in the talk therapy model, and that gives therapists a constant challenge. But many (even most) people are already excessively externally referenced, tending to be so dependent on other people's appreciation or acceptance that it actually hinders their own self-expression or identity.

Most therapists acknowledge that it can be very hard to work with a client who is highly externally referenced, either because their issues tend to be framed as other people's fault, expecting others to change, and they are typically unwilling or lack the skill and experience to look at themselves, or because they are so concerned about other people's opinions that they are unable to make a move for themselves.

Unfortunately, as we have seen, the unequal power relationship is likely to give the client a starting perspective that is already externally referenced. And because they are broken in themselves and do not possess the resources to be whole, they need a "power greater than ourselves to restore us to sanity."

Let's look at what happens when a client has to deal with external intervention.

The pattern I see is that the client must constantly switch from paying attention to their own internal reality, ideas, needs, and thoughts, to the therapist's reality, ideas, needs, and thoughts and back again.

Take a simple example. Even a seemingly innocuous request such as "Tell me more about that" actually introduces multiple external ideas.

The first is the idea of *me*, which pushes the *therapist's* identity and intentions into the client's consciousness.

Second, the statement implies that *there is more to tell*, and, third, that to participate properly in therapy requires saying *more about that*. It would not be surprising, therefore, for a client to expend effort to try to come up with the thing that the therapist has commanded them to come up with.

I can see how a client may find it difficult to attend to what is happening for them at the same time as attending to the therapist. They must constantly make the effort to move their focus inside-outside-inside-outside, potentially asking themselves if they are saying the right thing?

To extend this idea only slightly, it is not uncommon for therapy clients to take on the concern of what the therapist wants to hear. This may come from second-guessing the therapist's own wants. Taking the concept still further, we get into the realm of phenomena like false memory syndrome, which we can acknowledge is very harmful.

The pattern of continually pulling the client's awareness out of their own reality and into someone else's reality may hinder their progress. But it also pushes responsibility for progress onto the therapist.

I realized many years ago that I don't really want to be responsible for somebody else's decisions in life any more than I'm happy for a therapist to be responsible for mine. How can I know what's best for another person? Can any amount of training make us right all the time, or even *any* of the time?

Most of the therapists I know are also not comfortable with the idea of taking responsibility for their clients, but while they believe they do everything possible to keep the focus on the client's own processes, the reality is that their methods and the nature of the relationship require them to try to provide solutions.

Therapists often also report that this responsibility is fatiguing. The concept of "holding the space" for clients (as though we need to create a magical force field and maintain it through willpower) takes a significant amount of energy. Then, trying to figure out what is best, what is working, what is not working, what they should say next, how they can help this person... this all takes a lot of effort (and may also disconnect the therapist from being able to listen fully).

Emotional exhaustion is acknowledged to be a risk of the profession, particularly when dealing with the effects of trauma for prolonged periods. Sensitive people are more susceptible. It explains the relatively high occurrence of stress, depression, and substance abuse among therapists. In addition, burnout can result in detachment and therefore substandard service, which is unethical (this article[13] lists fifteen professional hazards that can contribute to therapists' burnout).

A 1988 study[14] reported that a survey of 562 licensed, doctoral-level, practising psychologists found "more than a third of the sample reported experiencing high levels of both emotional exhaustion and depersonalization."

"The Stresses of Counselling in Action" (SAGE, Windy Dryden, ed.) shares the conclusions of previous research...

> "Farber (1990) summarized his research on therapist burnout by concluding that therapists become burnt out when their work does not, ultimately, "pay off." While therapists expect a fair amount of stress in their daily work, they also expect to reap benefits that compensate for their efforts. Farber found that lack of therapeutic success was the most stressful part of counsellors' work..."

We might agree that externalizing responsibility is necessary for progress to happen in an expert-client scenario. But do the results validate the methods? Could it be that the constant switching between internal and external perspectives simply doesn't work for some clients? Is progress really not possible without it?

We are left with picture of therapy that embodies *yang* energy: active and dominant. Despite the fact that the majority of psychotherapists working today are female. Are our basic methods inherently more masculine in nature? Perhaps there is a place for more *yin* energy in therapy, which would be softer, less direct, and less controlling.

This prompts us to enquire how we might rearrange the client-expert relationship such that the client gets to stay more within their own psychic space, while the expert remains outside, and where the client can follow their own process, guided and supported but *not unduly influenced* by the expert's language, personal preferences or unsolicited suggestions.

6. Dependency

The picture we're building seems rife with conflicts and contradictions. As therapists we want to help clients, but there are several features intrinsic to our methods that might hinder our ability to do so.

We start with an unequal power relationship that makes it easy for clients to abdicate responsibility to the therapist. We have been taught to operate in the realm of brokenness using intrusive methods, which can have a knock-on effect of opening up other problems, and we do that often with no clear agreed goal for ending the therapy.

Let's examine further the problem of *the end of therapy*. In the spirit of inquiry, we should look at ourselves and ask an important but challenging question...

"What part do we play in fostering dependency on therapy?"

Clearly, drug manufacturers are faced with an economic conflict of interest. They get revenue when people take the drugs they make. If the drugs resulted in rapid and complete recovery, that might damage their revenue streams. (It is often said that the pharmaceutical industry "doesn't create cures, it creates customers.")

Is there a similar natural conflict of interest for therapists? When we are in the therapy business, when clients continue to pay for treatment for weeks, months, even years without achieving a satisfactory outcome, it might not seem to be in our interests to question why. Is it really in your personal interests for clients not to need therapy anymore? What would happen if your clients could come and see you for two sessions, and then never need to see you again? Perhaps that is even a threatening idea.

In a market that is gradually shrinking, might therapists be inclined to encourage their clients' dependency on them, whether deliberately or unconsciously? Are therapists dependent on recurring "cash cow" revenue from clients stuck in a habit of therapy without solution? Does the noble desire to get clients out of therapy as soon as possible conflict with our own natural desire for security?

We all naturally crave security for ourselves and our families. It is one of our deepest, most visceral animal urges, rooted deep in our limbic brains. Whereas, for most of us, daily survival and comfort are a given, that instinct latches on to money as a buffer against destitution and even death. It would therefore be perfectly natural and understandable if the prospect of facing and challenging our own dependency on recurring clients causes fear.

I think there may be another factor at work in the way therapy is practised that could further encourage a therapist to retain clients whom they may not be able to serve further. That is the problem of asking for referrals. Whereas a coach or holistic practitioner may freely request and welcome personal referrals by their clients, it is frowned upon in the therapy sector, even illegal in many States. That leaves therapists passively waiting for clients to come to them, rather than actively pursuing new business, resulting in increased financial dependency on existing clients.

This anecdote comes directly from a licensed therapist I work with...

> I have a client I've seen for almost 2 years who has seen several other therapists for "depression" for almost ten years. She had recently told me that she was feeling worse (and certainly had not been showing any improvement).
>
> Now, I suspected from the beginning that this client was only in therapy to maintain government benefits (welfare, disability, etc.) When she told me that she was feeling even more depressed, I told our agency director that I should refer her to someone else... since she wasn't progressing. His initial response was that he didn't see a problem and that I could continue seeing her because "we had a good relationship developed."
>
> Now, understand that the standard of care is that if

a depressed client isn't improved in 5 sessions, they should be referred, according to some experts on depression. But this agency director felt that there was no need to terminate... To me that's an example of how little we're taught how and when to terminate therapy appropriately.

It could be argued that, because therapists benefit by encouraging clients' dependency on therapy, they risk falling into a codependent relationship, not too dissimilar to the way a drug dealer fosters the addiction cycle: use > abuse > dependency > addiction.

Would it be appropriate to apply the addiction cycle to therapy use?

Some people **use** therapy periodically, just to clear their own head. My own partner is happy to visit a therapist every now and again "just to talk it out." That kind of use is no different to enjoying the occasional glass of wine or needing to go for a walk to get personal space.

Abuse is the start of the slippery slope. We might define abuse as feeling compelled to use something in situations where you ought to be expected to cope without that thing. So saying, "I need a couple of glasses of wine so that I can relax in the evening," might be an early sign of the start of alcohol abuse. In a therapeutic model this may sound something like "I need to see my therapist before making this decision or taking action."

Dependency is pretty clear. There is some kind of withdrawal when the thing is not available. Dependency might be expressed as, "I can't get through the day without my cigarettes." Alternatively, a person may not feel she is able to "be herself" in normal situations without the prop.

In terms of therapy, dependency would take the form of a person, who does not have a clear clinical need, feeling consistently concerned about their ability to deal with seemingly normal events in their life to the point where they can not manage without turning to a therapist for direction or validation. That is by no means an extraordinary scenario to consider. This woman's story is not unusual.

> *I began therapy for physical ailments and continued to go to the same therapist for the next 10 years. First it began as a way of coping with my ailments and continued on for other reasons — kids, marriage, personal difficulties and eventually to checking with my therapists for everyday decision making "I had better check with X before I / we ..." to do with ordinary family and relationship stuff.*

> *It just accelerated over time averaging about 18 appointments or more a year, depending on what was happening.*

> *I began to refer to my therapist as my 'close friend" although she, my therapist, never saw me outside of the therapy room. During this time I was also referred to other psychological professionals that could diagnose and prescribe medications for what my therapist saw as depression and anxiety.*

> *This led to a ten year spiral of not getting better, and a string of medications so long I ended up see a pharmaceutical specialist just to sort through all my medication — from both psychiatric and medical professionals — to look at the cumulative impact. And not being able to go for very long without getting a therapist's feedback and approval on my next steps, the burden on my spouse and family was terrible.*

> *We have since moved and I have stopped seeing this therapist now and still it feels like I have lost something. It feels like I have lost a close friend. And I am not sure what I am going to do now.*

The line between dependency and **addiction** is subjective.

Only an addict can say if they're an addict, when they admit the fact that they need the next fix so much that they will go to extreme lengths to get it. We might imagine a scenario where a client may need some external stimulus in order to function, such as understanding or validation, and which they believe they can only get in the therapy room.

There is clearly a natural risk of dependency for certain clients, for whom therapy may seem to offer the opportunity to continue to play the role of a child (i.e. externalizing responsibility). In this way, therapy could easily be *used* to replace one type of neediness with another.

Aside from externalizing responsibility to an authority figure, what other factors might clients find in the therapy room that could contribute to dependency? Could the brokenness paradigm subtly encourage some individuals to abdicate responsibility in their own lives, by reinforcing cause-and-effect? If that creates a bubble of victimhood with no responsibility, it is conceivable that a client may feel compelled to *use therapy* to maintain the belief structure, thereby creating the conditions for dependency.

A further scenario that might risk promoting dependency is where the client is not showing progress (in the therapist's view), and the therapist resorting to suggesting more therapy as the only possible solution.

I'm sure I don't know one therapist who would consciously encourage a client's dependency. The therapists I know don't enjoy the dependency, but don't have any other way. It is generally accepted that dependency comes with the territory.

We must admit it introduces an unpleasant paradox, in which a person may approach a professional for "healing", but in an economic environment that is set up in such a way as to discourage the professional from delivering their intended result as quickly as they might.

At the very least, we may acknowledge the risk of an ethical dilemma. I also think there exists the *potential* for encouraging dependency, built right into the economic model. The issues I have highlighted so far could all contribute to a scenario where a client might feel they face two unpleasant alternatives, either...

A. Endless therapy, which they do not have the power or confidence to end;

B. Or taking the decision to walk out, which might mean admitting failure, and potentially fearing negative consequences.

Whether we are able to resist the temptation to indulge dependent clients, and assuming we would never seek to nurture it, the talk therapy model seems to bring with it an intrinsic risk of dependency. That may explain why so many books have been written on the topic of how to end a course of therapy.

Is there a better way? Is it possible to conceive of a model where the client bears full responsibility for their own progress, where externalized responsibility is not fostered, and where dependency cannot take hold?

How do the Six Factors Contribute to the Failure of Therapy?

When we put all these factors together, is it surprising that therapy only works some of the time, or only for some people?

Is the fact that the different models have curiously consistent success rates a positive sign of its broad effectiveness, or could it be that it represents instead a predictable failure rate — a ceiling that talk therapy seems unable to break through?

I suggest it may be possible that each of these common challenges is responsible for, or contributes to, the failure of talk therapy for a certain subset of clients, *irrespective of what school of therapy is being practised.*

- Maybe *some people* are unable to access their own abilities and desires within an unequal power relationship.

- Maybe *some of us* cannot find wholeness when operating in the realm of brokenness, seeking out and reiterating painful memories, perhaps susceptible to cross-contamination.

- Perhaps intrusive methods that dig up and revisit old hurts just don't work for *some personality types.*

- Could it be that *certain individuals* need a clear goal to work towards, and cannot get on with a process that lacks something to aim for, and has no definition of success?

- Maybe *some clients* struggle to accept responsibility for their choices and their lives within the context of a client-expert relationship that forces them continually to move their frame of reference outside of themselves.

- Is it possible that a *certain group of clients* is happy to use therapy as a way of avoiding having to take sovereign responsibility, while another finds it impossible to break out of dependency on an authority figure?

In summary, psychotherapy has been founded on the belief that the path to healthy and whole thinking is not already present in the client, and therefore external expert intervention is required in order to effect the desired change.

Instead of persisting the myth of the resistant or incapable client, we might speculate whether the method of trying to empower a certain proportion of clients in the context of a disempowered client-expert relationship simply doesn't always work.

I want you now to visualize a model for psychotherapy that is free of these shortcomings.

Envisioning a Cleaner Model: Six Vital Signs

How can therapists find a way to work differently with their clients that helps create real, lasting results for their clients, without the endemic shortcomings we have seen in classical psychotherapy?

Can we imagine a therapy that functions without the need for an unequal power relationship, without intrusive methods, without needing to operate in the realm of brokenness, which uses clearly defined desired outcomes, where responsibility does not need to be shifted from the client, and where the environment encourages the development of healthy autonomy and individuation?

Let's revisit the six fundamental factors, imagine what it would take to move forward without them, and what that would mean to our practice.

1. The Client is Empowered

What would therapy look like if power *did not shift* from the client to the therapist?

Can you even have therapy without a therapist who *carries out analysis* using a complex model or DSM diagnosis, and who then goes on to *deliver remedies*?

To consider that would require acknowledging that the therapist may help *create the conditions for change*, but they do not *create the change itself*.

I have no doubt that, in order to get into a receptive state, it is extremely beneficial to have someone direct *your* attention, helping you to remain focused on your desired outcome. Without direction you may just be daydreaming. The question is, can the professional facilitator help the client to achieve their desired outcomes without assuming a position of authority?

Therapy today follows the *top-down pattern*, where the authority who has skill disperses some of that skill to someone with less skill. This patriarchal (*yang*) model is shared with many other disciplines that have their roots in the Industrial Revolution era, including education, publishing, and religion. It has been the de facto model since Freud's era a century ago, despite the fact that the majority of psychotherapists practising in this country today are women.

Recently, though, many sectors have found that alternative *bottom-up models* can also be effective. (We could look at Ken Robinson's presentations on new paradigms in public education,[15] where he advocates structuring education around the individual child, as an example.) Could there be a parallel, more bottom-up paradigm that might work for psychotherapy?

If so, it would have to be one in which the capacity and the structure for wellness come from the client, not from an external model provided by the expert.

I believe this is the key question:

> *Does the client possess the resources to have the life they want?*

If the solution can only be extrinsic, the method must therefore be extrinsic, and intrusive. But if the solution can be sourced intrinsically, we can — and should — find a way to work intrinsically.

That would require a radical re-evaluation of the fundamental tenet of psychotherapy that broken clients need external intercession in order to become well, moving to one where the capacity for healthy thinking is intrinsic to every human being.

The mode of therapy would also need to shift significantly.

Instead of suggesting solutions, we would need to create a space where it is acknowledged that the client already has the potential to get the outcomes they want in their life, and that it is the therapist's role to support them to realize that possibility.

2. Victimless Therapy

What would therapy look like if we did not introduce concepts like *victim*, *perpetrator*, *trauma*, and *abuse*?

Are these constructs really necessary to achieve healing and personal growth? Or can we reach our ideal destination without passing through the realm of brokenness?

I believe the phenomenon of *retraumatization* shows us that the realm of brokenness is not a healthy environment. In fact, I would go further and say that continually digging into old wounds cannot help scars to heal.

The possibility of victimless therapy pivots on another important question that we have already touched on...

Does understanding alone cause change?

Understanding causes understanding, but that does not necessarily result in change. Stating the facts of past events might facilitate acceptance, but positive change surely demands more than acceptance, otherwise it would be much easier to achieve, and more common.

We can create cause-and-effect structures, but how are those structures useful? For example, I may *understand* that I flinch every time I hear a loud noise, and then I may come to *understand* through therapy that I have that physical reaction *because* my father suddenly hit me from behind when I was six.

I use the term "*becausation*", taken from Penny Tompkins and James Lawley, to describe that kind of cause-and-effect construct when used in a therapeutic context. Does repeating the becausation make it less powerful, or more powerful? And does understanding the becausation enable me to *change* the way I react?

I am not saying that becausations are bad or wrong. They can actually be very powerful, but only *if you're on the cause side!* To be on the effect end of a becausation is to be a victim. But to be on the cause end is powerful and liberating, e.g. "I choose to do this because I am..."

But I do find that becausations are often counter-productive because of the ritual effect caused by repetition. Where is the liberation in, "I'm a nervous person because my father hit me" or "I have trouble trusting men because my father hit me"?

These beliefs are the logical glue that hold our perceptions in space and time, but that does not make them true or useful. Of course, the more we repeat these causes and effects as truths, the more they seem to *appear* to be true. It is a physiological fact that thoughts create neural pathways in the cerebellum that are reinforced every time the thought is repeated. But no amount of reinforcement makes ideas any more *true*, and if they are not true, then why would resolving them result in positive change?

In my experience, becausations will tell you a lot about a person's logic, and will show you how they justify their behavior, but I cannot honestly give you one example where a becausation about a historical event has directly caused — or even enabled — change.

Past events are past events, but change can only happen in the present moment. Using the previous example, what might happen *in the present moment* is: I feel my breath catch; I feel my shoulders raise; then I remember by father. There is a cause-effect happening in the present: "When this happens, I react in that way." That is something that can be changed. However, the historical cause-effect: "I am this way because my father did that," is something we probably cannot change as long as it is stated as a fact.

These historical becausations lock our thinking into being at *effect*, which is disempowering and very different from an *at cause* pattern such as, "Because I am strong and resourceful, I can..."

Instead of continually constructing a model of abuse and victimhood, what if we were to start therapy from the point of view that *there is nothing wrong*? And, if the client thinks there is something wrong, we don't see anything wrong in that either.

What we have is a model of how a person works. There is a stimulus, which is followed by a sequence of reactions. This all makes sense. The person is working exactly the way that people work. She is whole, not broken. (And, being systemic, if the client comes in and says, "I'm broken," then that is where we start. And when you are broken, what would you like to have happen?)

And... what she would like to have happen is to be able to experience that kind of stimulus and have a different sequence of reactions follow.

Now, what if we are able to see and treat this human being as fully capable, regardless of their past and present difficulties?

In cognitive linguistics, this sequence of events is called *body cognition*. The realization that those triggers are connected with those reactions gives me what might be termed an *associative context*, or what Benjamin Bergen calls a *simulation of an event*. I prefer to use the term *model*, which simply means a *way of understanding and describing the way something works*. (To learn more about this type of cognition, I recommend Benjamin Bergen's book "Louder Than Words", 2012.)

Having a model is a first step toward being able to create

lasting change, by associating those triggers with a different outcome in the present moment.

Let me share a personal example where I used models creatively to change my real present experience.

For much of my life, I had difficulty with my mother's communication. Whenever she gave me advice, I would feel a sense of being burdened with something that I couldn't get away from.

I realized that, to me, my mother's words were like sticky burrs, the ones covered with tiny hooks that stick to your clothing and are troublesome to remove. That was my *model*: a representation of what the experience of being with my mother was like for me.

However, once I had that realization, I was able to make a choice. When I was going over this with a colleague, what occurred to me was what I wanted to have happen is for my mother's words no longer to be sticky burrs, but become instead drops of lead, which dropped from her tongue straight onto the ground at her feet. And that gave me another choice. I could choose to pick up the words and take ownership of them, or I could leave them where they lay.

In that moment I created a *new model* — one which worked better for me — and the old model was discarded.

Here is what is important about that *remodeling*. My mother did not change. In fact, she didn't need to change, because there was nothing wrong. There was only the awareness that the way I reacted to her communication was not the way I wished to react. I was not a victim, and she was not wrong. All the change happened in my own perception.

If we, as professionals, do not need to introduce the structure of brokenness, what does that leave us to work with?

For most psychotherapy models, we would need to introduce a radically different paradigm, which requires no judgement about broken or sick. Things would simply be as they are. The context for our work can only then be, how would the client prefer things to be and what needs to happen for them to have that? And, in the context of the client who already possesses the capacity to create that change, our work would become a process of facilitating the client's own intrinsic potential for change.

3. Unintrusive

This then leads naturally to a model that does not require intrusive methods and their associated risk of cross-contamination.

If we accept that the client possesses the facility to create change, and that there is nothing wrong or broken, all that is required is to allow the change to happen from within: which means that we must use *intrinsic methods* working with the client's subjective experience and how they express that, rather than extrinsic intervention.

I believe that intrinsic methods are already available and practised in all forms of talk therapy. Whenever we ask a client a truly open question, we introduce nothing yet we may discover more. That is knowledge and capability intrinsic to the client.

The problem is that it is so easy to step into intervention. After all, that is our default model. I find that even most "open" questions can be leading.

Some techniques, including creative visualization or hypnotherapy, might appear to be free from the usual shortcomings, but they are still therapist-led. If the therapist creates the alternative vision, using their metaphor or story, that may or may not be meaningful or helpful to the client.

Take this real example of what happened to Zoe, an acquaintance of mine who was leading a group in a visualization she had used many times before.

I often use the example of creating a beach scene, a common one for guided visualization. You would think, how that can be dangerous? It sounds benign doesn't it? On one occasion, I ended with a guided meditation and sound healing. Afterwards, one of the women in the group physically could not get up off the floor! She needed someone to come and pull on her leg to help her stand up. She then told me that she suffered from PTSD and when I mentioned being on a beach in my visualization it triggered her. She said before I do meditations like that I should really ask if people have any traumas I should be aware of. Now I know.

This is such a seemingly innocuous example, yet it shows us that anything that a therapist or facilitator introduces could trigger undesired consequences. The idea of "beach" was not a helpful resource for this particular woman, for some reason. Of course, the facilitator couldn't have known that in advance. We can never reliably predict what will be harmless, or what will be traumatic.

An alternative model would require that the facilitator stay outside of the client's psychic space, so maintaining the client's integrity. The client would then leave the session with nothing new added, and nothing taken away, only what they brought in with them, and what they had personally discovered and realized.

4. Setting Desired Outcomes

We have seen that goal-less therapy can become an end in itself, leading naturally to endless treatment and even dependency. Many people simply go and "get therapy" without a goal or remedy in mind.

In my own experience, without a clearly defined outcome, and rooted in the realm of brokenness, therapy simply becomes an endless process of digging up more trash to process.

For therapy to be objectively successful, it helps to have two things: some definition of what success means; and a way to recognize when it has been reached.

Without that measure or guide, it falls to the expert therapist to navigate, using their own evaluation of progress or success.

How can a client expect to get a positive result from therapy without having some idea of where they want to go? I believe they need an outcome, in the form of some sensory or internal experience that they're driving for, which lets them *know* that things are better.

I will often spend half of the first session helping my client define "what they want to have happen." It is really surprising how many people have never been asked that question before. Once we the client has stated their desired outcome, that becomes the basis of our agreed shared objective. It is also the measure I use to know when sessions are moving toward a positive outcome, or if we need to adjust the course.

Keeping such a strong emphasis on desired outcome requires that I listen actively, because the client may share information or use language that indicates their desired outcome may have shifted or developed during the session, or even change from session to session as the client finds out more about what they want to have happen and its ecological effect on other parts of their life.

I believe that our deepest desires are almost always *intrinsic*. I have seen many clients who come with a particular conscious externalized want (for example, status or a relationship), but when they work through their hopes and dreams freely. Something that happens for many clients is often what they most deeply desire comes down to a *way of being*.

In my own experience, it is extremely worthwhile taking that time to discover the client's desired outcome. Sure, any therapist can issue a diagnosis and prescribe what the client should be aiming for, but that goal, and the methods used to achieve it, would be *extrinsic* to the client, stuck in the old model that holds that change is only possible through expert intervention.

We should commit to engaging in therapy exclusively in the context of a clearly defined outcome that is created by and owned by the client.

5. Enhancing Responsibility

Let's look at the idea of the "resistant client" for a moment. I'm not saying the phenomenon isn't real, rather that it isn't helpful. If we agree that it is possible for a client to be resistant, and that *that* resistance can thwart the efforts of the therapist or due to that resistance clients thwarting their own efforts, what does that tell us about how therapy works?

Could it simply be the case that we do not have the tools for dealing with this scenario?

Where therapy succeeds (as it often does, even in the classical model built on an unequal power relationship, using dirty and intrusive methods, operating in the realm of brokenness, and with no agreed goal), one thing remains true: *The client must actively participate*. Without the client's involvement, no therapy can work.

I would ask you to consider the possibility that it is actually *clients* who implement successful therapy. If that could be the case, it must only happen when the method is compatible with the client. That in turn might explain the steady failure rate we see across the board: because certain types of people may find certain shortcomings of traditional talk therapy unworkable.

If it is the case that some clients are able to use the therapist's interventions successfully to effect their own change, if we could use a model that actively enhanced the client's responsibility, that might make it possible to achieve higher success rates.

Clearly, a first step must be for the client to own their own outcome. If the goal point is prescribed by someone else, the client does not own it. So it may only make sense and be accessible to the client within the context of the therapy sessions.

But when the client creates and owns their desired outcome, and when they realize that they are at state-of-being "A" but wish to be at state-of-being "B", it becomes clear that what is needed is some change in state-of-being. Furthermore, that shift, through attention to their desired outcome, will seem to be within their own capability and that ownership will systemically extend to their future decisions and behavior patterns.

The start point is the client's. The desired end point is the client's. The metaphorical path from one point to the other is their own. Only the client can choose to walk it. And, ultimately, only they can say when they have reached the place they wished to reach.

In this emerging alternative model, the power to create change resides within the client's psychic space. They require no permission from an interceding expert. It is a simple act of personal, sovereign choice. I cannot overstate the importance of this ownership, not least because the client may take their own vision and desire with them outside the therapy room.

If the present state, the desired state, and the path between the two, are intrinsic to the client, surely they have all they need to make the required changes.

A healthier model of therapy, which could work for everyone, would both honor and develop the client's responsibility over their life.

6. Honoring The Client's Freedom

After leaving college, I went to Los Angeles to study music. Since I had come across this latent memory and started the whole therapeutic process back at college in Montana, I ended up continuing with therapy in Los Angeles.

I already knew I was not interested in therapy as external soothing, and I found myself drawn towards hypnotherapy and Jungian psychology.

It was around that time when I got a taste of how somebody else's models can be both highly influential and also potentially damaging to a client. Let me share an example from my own experience.

The school I was studying in had its own theories about dreams. I had one particular dream, in which I was in a deep pool. It was set in a beautiful setting, like a quarry, with small edges around the pool, surrounded by tall cliffs.

There was another girl in the pool with me, who was kind of like me. In the dream we just swam and floated. It felt comfortable and intimate. It didn't have a sexual connotation to me, more like the young woman in my dream was a reflection of myself. I took this to my hypnotherapist and she said, "Hmm, I think that you have latent lesbian urges."

I was very surprised, but trusted that she knew what she was doing, because she had been doing this kind of therapy for a long time. I took my therapist's analysis really seriously and decided I should look at it. I spent about a year closely examining my feelings about other women, whether I found their bodies beautiful or interesting. Eventually, I concluded that, although I found the female form beautiful, I was not sexually attracted to women.

I am not saying I regret going down that path, I did learn something about myself, but I know it would not have happened had I not been dependent on the therapist's external diagnosis or analysis, which sowed that seed in my mind. And perhaps that year might have been better spent learning about something more helpful or nourishing to me. If I hadn't been the person I am, I could have taken what she said as fact, and acted on it, in a way that might not have proven beneficial for me.

As a client, I kept going into these therapeutic sessions thinking that I was going to feel better and be doing better, but I didn't. I didn't know if it was the tool or the therapist, but after about six months, I decided that hypnotherapy was not giving me what I wanted. I also realized *I was getting a lot of things that I hadn't asked for*.

Later, as I was going through my own training in hypnosis and NLP, I noticed that people would come to me and almost seem to serve themselves up to me on a platter, as though they were saying, "Here I am, put me under and fix me."

I found it incredibly tiring having to be so clever all the time, having to come up with the stories and scenarios I thought would work for my clients. Something didn't feel right. It felt like I was constantly pushing against something, and I had a deep concern I couldn't shake that what I was doing was somehow manipulative and not quite right for my client.

I realize now that I was looking for a method that did not depend on having an external expert who provides the answers. I know I am someone who does not like to be told what to do and I don't like to tell others what to do. Maybe my having that personality type is why all these models of therapy have ultimately failed me.

But I could not find a form of therapy that did not require some kind of dependency on that outside expert stance, where the client could set the rules and decide what they wanted and when the therapy was complete.

That model, if it did exist, would naturally be more immune from dependency and the risk of addiction, because it would be the client who creates and owns the process, and who possesses the ability to find their own answers.

Exploring Other Worlds

I stopped doing hypnosis, and I stepped back from psychology for a while. I did continue to complete my Bachelor's degree, all the time thinking, "Maybe there are some models in traditional psychology that will make more sense." As I've always been fascinated with the symbolic realm and have been cataloging my dreams since I was fourteen, it seemed natural I focused on Jungian analysis.

Around that time I also started mentoring in shamanic "journey" work under a Matis elder, which also deals in the realm of symbology. This would involve traveling to a symbolic "lower world" on a client's behalf and bring back resources for them, which might be a feather, a colored crystal, a water droplet, or some other object. Under the guidance of the elder, I would then place these resources in or around the person's body using my breath.

What I liked about the shamanic work was that we would bring back these resources but never told the client *what these resources were supposed to mean to them*, even if we had our own theory about it. We just placed the allegorical objects, but then let the client find their own meaning and experience.

Although it still depended on the intercession of an external party (the shaman), I liked that this work honored the client's ability to assign meaning to the objects themselves.

Shamanism has a respectable place in some forms of Jungian therapy. The key difference is, where Jungian analysis works with the collective unconscious and *archetypal symbols*, shamanic methods work with the client's idiosyncratic *subjective*. We often referred to what we brought back as *pieces of themselves*, *resources*, or *tools*.

In my experience, having used both approaches, archetypes and subjective, I believe each may be helpful on some level, but I believe it is the subjective that can lead to change in ways that are both more immediate and more visible and actionable in our day to day lives.

For example, I had a dog that would appear in my dreams. Working with my Jungian analyst, we looked at what dogs represent in the archetypal realm. But that just didn't fit for me. In my dream, the dream dog felt like the complete opposite. *My* dog, in *my* dream meant something specific to *me*, in relationship to what I knew about dogs, the breed that appeared and my years of personal experience owning large breeds.

The archetypal meaning didn't feel right to me, like only half an answer. That's when I realized that working with a person's *subjective symbology* is crucially important to getting their view, experience and understanding of the world.

I believe that if you want lasting change to happen, you need to work with a person's internal, subjective experience. It is our intrinsic model — the way we understand the world — that fundamentally impacts the way we relate to our world. Changes that come from the outside, whether from an external model or the suggestions of an expert, will only be real to us if we can make them our own.

I continued the shamanic work for over ten years, however I couldn't shake the feeling that there was something further to discover. If people really possess the ability to use symbols and ideas to effect the change they want, why should they need a third party to provide those symbols? Could there be a better way?

Stumbling on a More Beautiful Question

After my decades of therapy, training, and spiritual exploration, the breakthrough I had been looking for came from the most unlikely source.

I had gone back to doing therapeutic work and was working to set up my own therapy and coaching business, but it was taking time to develop my client base, so I started working with Weight Watchers™ to supplement my income.

In my role as a Weight Watchers leader, I was required to attend a training, held about sixty miles from where I lived. I went reluctantly, but it was at that meeting that I was introduced to five simple questions. They were presented to us as a tool that might be helpful in our interactions with people hoping to lose weight. Those questions changed the course my career and my life. The questions were...

> *"What would you like to have happen?"*
>
> *"What needs to happen?"*
>
> *"Is there anything else that needs to happen?"*
>
> *"Can you..?"*
>
> *"Will you..?"*

Something about the purity of those short questions seemed to connect with something deep down in my consciousness. They somehow fit beautifully for me.

I later learned that the first four questions were taken from something called *Clean Language* and the last one came from *Motivational Interviewing*. I had not heard of Clean Language before, but I knew in my gut that there was something different about these questions than anything I had come across before.

As soon as the training was over I got in the car, drove home, and went straight online to find out more. What I discovered exceeded my expectations.

From the moment I started reading about Clean Language, it was as if I was meeting an entire community that thought like me! Here were people talking about how we use metaphors in speech to explain our experiences. What's more, they had a method for working with those metaphors and symbols that has proven effective in many contexts, including therapy, but using subjective symbols — not archetypal theory.

At first, Clean Language seems incredibly simple The facilitator uses a set of around ten core questions, in conjunction with repeating what the client says back to them, to help the client express what's going on for them and what they would like to have happen. Two simple rules: only use clean questions and only repeat back your clients words verbatim.

The remarkable thing about Clean Language — and the reason it was called "clean" — is the facilitator only uses "clean" questions together with the *client's own exact words*. They introduce no ideas, concepts, or metaphors of their own. So the word "clean" is a metaphor for the questions being "cleaned" as far as possible of assumptions and presuppositions. In this way, the idea is that this creates an environment in which the client can begin to *work out for themselves* what they want, and what needs to happen for them to get it.

I recognized that Clean Language was compatible with models I was already working with, like the landscape of a client's personal "lower world", their intrinsic, subjective symbolic resources, and this idea of how we use symbols and archetypes in our thinking. But I soon realized it went much further, applying new learning from the fields of *cognitive linguistics*, *cognitive science*, and *self-organizing systems theory*. The more I read about Clean Language, the more the pieces seemed to come together.

At that time, in late 2005, Clean Language was virtually

unheard of in the United States. Two leaders in the field were Penny Tompkins and James Lawley, who were in the UK.

I ordered their book, *Metaphors in Mind*, and their video, *A Strong and Strange Sensation*, and immediately started using their methodology, Symbolic Modeling, in sessions with my clients. I was excited to get going, because it seemed so elegant — and so easy! But I quickly figured out that, although it seemed simple, I could only follow the process for about four questions before running into a wall of complexity. There seemed to be many subtleties in working with another individual using their idiosyncratic language that I didn't understand.

Within two weeks of trying Clean Language, I had signed myself onto my first two-day training course in the UK to learn the first steps. I loved it! As soon as I got back home to California I thought, "I want more of this!"

That was the start of two years traveling to training courses in Europe, for just two or three days at a time, culminating in a six-day training in France July 2007, where I became the first certified Clean Facilitator under the supervision of Penny Tompkins and James Lawley.

At first I thought I would blend Clean Language with other things I was currently doing. As it is a neutral tool that can be easily done, but what I found over time was, as my skills with Clean Language increased, my need and interest in blending with other methods diminished, simply because these methods were so flexible and so consistently effective.

I think the reason I immediately switched on to working with Clean Language was because it allowed me to be all the things I wanted to be: a skilful observer, a curious interviewer, and a logical thinker. But what I *didn't have to do* was to be clever, or to offer solutions! That is a subtle but important distinction.

For someone like me, that was a huge relief. I also noticed

that Clean Language sessions didn't leave me tired. In fact, as I started to witness clients coming up with their own solutions, the experience was actually *energizing*! I didn't have to "hold space", take on the client's difficulties, or provide pity or concern. It created a feeling of respect, capability and compassion instead. After each session, I really felt *clean*, without the need to release or shake off any stickiness psychically, as I had previously often experienced working with other systems.

To me, it felt like I'd found a method where I could help facilitate a person to take their own shamanic journey, but one in which they discover their own resources, they decide where those resources belonged, and what they mean to them. It felt like a perfect transition.

I think the highly disciplined principles and methods found in Clean Language could be the missing piece in some of the challenges that psychotherapy faces today.

Next, I'll describe how it works, show how it is robustly immune from the shortcomings of classic talk therapy, and explore how it might enhance the practice of therapy in the United States today.

A Cleaner Model

Clean Language was originally developed in the 1980s as a therapeutic tool by the psychologist David Grove. He was concerned with how even the most client-centered therapy models tended to introduce subtle changes to the client's own words, and how those changes affected the client and process of therapy. One of his principal concerns was how to avoid the impact of retraumatization in therapy.

David started to examine carefully the impact of even the slightest changes in the way therapists repeat their clients' language. This led him to begin to ask a different style of question. He also experimented with repeating a client's words back to them *verbatim*, carefully avoiding adding any new words or paraphrasing.

In addition to spoken language, he regarded metaphors, body language, and sounds as *literal communication*. Today, his theory is being validated by recent developments in cognitive linguistics, which shows that, in order to explain something that is abstract or complex, we frequently use metaphors that represent *embodied experiences*.

For example, if somebody says, "My back is against the wall," David would take that literally, as though that person was literally having the experience of their back against the wall. What's more, he maintained that the metaphors we use are idiosyncratic, such that "taking a leap into the dark" may represent a hopeful and positive action to one person but a terrifying loss of control to another.

David Grove believed that each of us possesses the answers to our own problems, and that we can discover those answers through a process of slowing down and focusing on our internal processes. For this to happen, it is necessary for the facilitator to remain outside the client's psychic space.l

David's work and unique style came to the attention of two NLP psychotherapists from the UK: Penny Tompkins and James Lawley. They went on to study in detail David's unique way of working with clients, and over a five-year period modeled his methods by recording his sessions, going over the transcripts, working directly with him as clients, as well as attending his trainings. Finally they had distilled David's methodology into a teachable model they called *Symbolic Modeling*.

Over the next ten years Clean Language (often used synonymously with Symbolic Modeling) slowly gained visibility in the UK, Continental Europe, and Australia. Sadly, David Grove passed in 2008 but his legacy has now lived on through James and Penny's and other people's work for over fifteen years.

In Clean Language, the facilitator's role is to help focus the client's attention on what is happening for them. Classic talk therapy is "client-centered": the therapist's focus, attention, and concern are directed towards the client. Clean Language, by contrast, could be described as "information-centered", being concerned with the client's relationship or rapport with their own information.

Clean Language also maintains a strong focus on the client's *desired outcome*, so a significant amount of time is initially invested expressing that outcome clearly. The facilitator must also be sensitive to noticing if the desired outcome evolves during or between sessions.

The desired outcome and personal metaphor is the pivot for the whole process. The facilitator's role is continually to guide the client's attention back to what they have expressed that they want. As that happens, the facilitator is developing a model of both the client's present experience and the experience they wish to have in epistemological metaphor (which simply means using the client's own individual vernacular and knowing).

Human communication and experience is metaphorical at its very core. We think and communicate using allegory and story. English language is absolutely packed with metaphor. In fact, it is estimated that English speakers commonly use at least one metaphor of some kind every six words. Metaphors help us to condense meaning, and the more complex the information, the more metaphor will tend to be used.

In the therapy room, whenever we put own metaphors and ideas into our communication with the client, and discard or change the language they use, we lose the majority of the content of their meaning. When that happens, how can we properly follow what they are saying? More importantly, how can *the client* keep on track with their own process?

In a "Clean" session, only the client's language and metaphors may be used. The facilitator must diligently avoid introducing their own metaphors, ideas, assumptions, opinions, or interpretations.

Below you can see the set of Clean questions originally created by David Grove. Understanding that "..." *may only ever be words that the client has previously provided*. You can see how these questions remain fixed on the client's desired outcome and internal landscape, using their own language and ideas.

> "And what kind of ... (is that ...)?"
>
> "And is there anything else about ...?"
>
> "And where is ...? or (And) whereabouts is ...?"
>
> "And that's ... like what?"
>
> "And is there a relationship between ... and ...?"
>
> "And when ..., what happens to ...?"
>
> "And then what happens?" (or "And what happens next?")

"And what happens just before ...?"

"And where could ... come from?"

"And what would ... like to have happen?" (often "And what would you like to have happen")

"And what needs to happen for ...?"

"And can ... (happen)?"

These questions permit minimal supposition. For example, there is no "Why..?" which might necessitate a reason (or becausation).

There is no question of veracity. The client's reality is the client's reality. It is real for them, with nothing to dispute. The process is simply like a spiral, focused exclusively on the client's truth, continually but gradually revealing their own personal reality.

In the next section, I will explore how Clean methods are naturally free from the six endemic weaknesses inherited by classic talk therapy models.

Freeing Talk Therapy From The Six Causes of Failure

"Talk" therapy by definition operates in the realm of language. The drawbacks that are intrinsic in the current therapeutic model must therefore also be linguistic, as must be any potential solution.

I will now explain how the Clean methodology is naturally free from each of the six factors that I believe may contribute to the failure of classic talk therapy.

Free from Unequal Power Relationship

As we have seen, the paradigm of classic psychotherapy is the assumption that the path to recovery does not belong to the client. They arrive broken and lacking the innate ability to become complete. Any possible path to recovery must start with analysis is delivered by an expert who is also qualified to prescribe solutions. This assigns all the power and responsibility to the therapist.

The Clean Language process is not therapy in itself. As we have seen, therapy is a *transitive* act that is practised on a person by an expert.

By contrast, Clean is *facilitated*.

> *A facilitator is someone who helps a group of people (usually, for us, a person) understand their common objectives and assists them to plan how to achieve these objectives; in doing so, the facilitator remains "neutral" meaning he/she does not take a particular position in the discussion.*[16]

Facilitation is not an end in itself. It adds nothing, but simply works with what is already there. We can extend that idea to say that the client must therefore necessarily bring with them everything they need.

A Clean facilitator does not really interact with the client, and does not deliver any change. They are more like a catalyst to enable change to happen, or a mirror, subtly reflecting the client's own concepts and model back to them. The facilitator makes no judgement about right or wrong, or assessment about how "well" sessions may be progressing.

In this way, the client remains the active party. Only they will choose their desired outcome, and only they will decide if and when it is met. The end result is zero transfer of power or control from client to facilitator.

Free from Operating in the Realm of Brokenness

Therapy is collapsing under the weight of its own diagnostics. Compare the growth of the Diagnostic and Statistical Manual of Mental Disorders (DSM), which in its fifth major edition now includes things like "Binge Eating Disorder" and "Generalized Anxiety Disorder". We should ask how having more and more diagnoses available really serves us.

By contrast, Clean does not diagnose, categorize, reduce, or label. The frame of reference is not "what's wrong". The only frame of reference is whether something is helpful to the client with regard to their desired outcome.

The absence of a brokenness paradigm is one of the ways that Clean Language relates to *Self-Organizing Systems Theory*, which sees the person as a whole, complete, functioning system, including past, future, and present. In fact, everything we do makes perfect sense in relationship to the history we carry.

The Clean methodology certainly does not require a victim. Of course we may work with words like "broken", "victim", or "wrong" — *if they come up in the client's language*. But, in the context of the client as a complete, working system, those are simply artefacts, metaphorical descriptions of a coherent internal experience.

In the absence of brokenness and "wrong", we are left with a point of view that everything a client does *makes perfect sense to them*, in the light of their experiences. Any meaning that the client attaches to events or people is therefore indisputable. The only context that matters is whether the client wants it or not.

As I mentioned previously, one of the primary reasons David Grove developed his way of working with clients was specifically to avoid retraumatization that can be caused by reliving the episode or events over and over all in the guise of increasing understanding. Part of David's theory is that people will speak of their trauma with gestures, sounds and metaphors as a way of expressing that does not exacerbate the trauma by allowing the client to communicate it in an encrypted way...

> *... a disciplined use of language that allows the information born of traumatic experience to be resolved and transformed. This approach values the infrastructure of clients language as the primary source that both defines the pathology and contains the seed of healing. Freeing the client's experience out of the secondary processing language of words (conceptual thinking and relating blow by blow events) into primary processing language of metaphor, symbol and imagery often brings the experience to life without re-traumatizing the client. The procedure makes the experience malleable and amenable to change. (David Grove & B.I. Panzer)*

If we are to accept that change can only happen in the choices of the present moment, we must reject the idea that understanding the past can drive change. So another important factor in Clean Language sessions is its focus on *present-time recognition*.

Clean facilitators do not use the past tense. Instead, they

will focus on events as though they are happening right now. Present-time recognition is based on the idea is that, as the client speaks of a past or imagined experience, in that speaking the experience is real for them in the room in that moment.

When we cease to dwell on past facts, and focus only on the present moment, we shift into a space that does not need pity or victimhood.

I saw a client who had been ritually physically and sexually abused as a pubescent girl by her father and other members of the satanic cult to which he belonged. I could have adopted the position of "Oh, how awful!" But this woman had had fifteen years of "Oh, how awful!" and it had not been useful for her.

I was also the first therapist who actually attended to "the father" — not *her father*. The distinction is subtle, but very powerful.

The construct, "When your father did that…" (in the past tense) takes her back into her past experience, where she can only passively re-experience painful events.

In contrast, "When *a father like that* does that…" uses the present tense. That simple change keeps us in the present moment, which of course is the only time choice and change can happen. Using "When a father like that, in a black cape, and a frown and a scowl… What would you like to have happen?" this client can begin to frame her world differently.

Unfortunately the beliefs from the past sometimes do not provide what is needed for the changes we need/want to make now.

Bringing the memories into present time brings all the change and maturity of a person to that memory. Through this a person can apply more of themselves toward their desired outcome.

Free from Intrusive Methods

As we have seen, Clean Language operates exclusively with internal reference. The process is designed first to help the client find that reference towards the outcome they want, and then to move towards their desired outcome by developing an embodied metaphor, to which they can return at any time.

An example of an embodied metaphor is my seeing my mother's words, which had previously been persistently uncomfortable for me, instead as drops of lead. The physical experience of the drops of lead being very different to the burrs that would attach themselves to me. I can imagine the drops of lead, the weight, color, feel as the fall towards the floor. That metaphor came from me, and it belongs to me, so I have it as a personal resource that I can access at any time.

I can share another personal example, which shows how persistent embodied metaphor can be. This actually came from my own very first Clean Language training ten years ago.

The metaphor (or embodied experience) is a coat rack, which is about six feet in front of me. It's one of those nice brown wood coat racks with the curled hooks. On the coat rack there is a "big girl" coat, and a "skin that I have to grow into" (all my words).

At the time I first created this picture, I didn't believe I could grow into that skin. And I believed the "big girl" coat, a coat made just for me, represented living up to my siblings and was related to my being given hand-me-down clothes.

About three years after I had this metaphor, as I continued working in Symbolic Modeling sessions, I had an embodied experience of growing into that skin. I also found my coat! I was on a shopping trip with some friends in LA, passed by a Lululemon shop and saw the coat in the window. Once I had tried it on I had to buy it, spending more on a coat than I ever thought possible. It is now a staple in my work wardrobe and when I put it on it has the taste of being just mine. In a way the metaphor became physicalized in my daily life. It could have been very easy to put this metaphor off as "just" an imaginary construct. After all who could have guessed that a coat rack, skin and coat could have so much lasting and intimate meaning for me?

This metaphor is still very real and alive for me, and it has completely shifted how I function as a capable, responsible grown-up in this world. I have no doubt that is part of why I have been able to achieve what I have in these past ten years.

The whole Clean Language methodology is based on the sure knowledge that each of us possesses the resources we need to get what we want. That expects — and also requires — that nothing should be introduced from outside. In fact, David Grove noticed that the slightest intrusion can derail a client from staying focused on their own processes.

As we have seen, it is extremely difficult for a therapist to keep outside of a client's psychic space. Even using language as seemingly innocent as, "How are you feeling today?" can add information to the context (starting with an implicit assumption that the client *should* be feeling something).

Of course, Clean Language must have some influence, but here James Lawley explains why it is important to keep the influence "clean"...

> *"Clean Language influences and directs attention — it wouldn't be useful if it didn't. However, unlike other uses of language, Clean Language is 'clean' because it is sourced in the client's exact vocabulary, it is consistent with the logic of their metaphors, and it only introduces universal metaphors of time, space, form, and perceiver."*[17]

When I give talks on the importance of the therapist keeping their own language and interpretations out of the client's head, I often hear therapists say, "You know, I do that." But in my experience, after working with and training therapists for over 9 years, even the most well-intentioned and focused cannot maintain that discipline, simply because it takes a special kind of training.

That is why the Clean Language methodology is so strict on using only "clean" questions, in order to keep the communication free of any leading, suggestion, or assumption. It is only through applying that discipline rigorously that we maintain the client's complete ownership, which I'm sure is the key to achieving consistent results.

Free from Goal-lessness

Our purpose as therapists is to help our clients to achieve what they want in their lives. But, as we know, therapy with no agreed goal risks becoming an endless process.

To have a relationship in which the client is fully empowered requires that they identify their own desired outcome, that they be the one to say if it changes at any point, and also be the one to decide if and when it is achieved.

In Clean Language and Symbolic Modeling, I mentioned we can sometimes spend half our time helping the client to discover their desired outcome. I find Seneca's famous aphorism helpful: "If a man does not know to what port he is steering, no wind is favorable to him." To put it in therapeutic language, without the frame of reference of a desired outcome, how can any of us discern what resources are helpful or unhelpful?

We also leave it to the client to decide whether their desired outcome is achievable or not. The facilitator does not make that determination. One reason is simply that we don't know what each person is capable of. A second reason is that outcomes are often expressed as individual metaphor, and we cannot break down what that means to the client.

When we focus our attention on what we want, that focus will determine the relevant memories, associations, and experience. So, in a Clean session, all questions are asked in relation to that desired outcome as the frame of reference. This enables the client to use ideas and metaphors that carry them towards where they wish to be.

A fascinating effect that many Clean practitioners have observed is that a client's expressed desired outcome can sometimes serve to deliver deeper outcomes, which may make sense in a metaphorical context.

For example, I had one client who was sad and was also drinking heavily. (She would occasionally tear up and at times I could smell alcohol on her breath.) In our first — and only — Symbolic Modeling session, her desired outcome was "cleaning up her house." She literally had boxes of receipts and paperwork in her house that she wanted to get rid of.

We did one session together and I did not see her again until she contacted me eighteen months later to tell me how profoundly life-changing that session had been for her. In that time, she had stopped drinking, revitalized her business, and gotten married! Maybe that's what "cleaning house" signified to this woman, on a subconscious symbolic level. What we do know is that, to her at that point in time, "cleaning house" was the appropriate desired outcome, so that's what we worked with.

Free from Externalizing Responsibility

Because Clean Language and Symbolic Modeling operate entirely within the client's own space, these methods not only make it hard for the client to externalize responsibility, but positively encourage a true awareness of responsibility. These words from a Clean therapy client describe the change...

> *Before I learned all this I could not care for myself or the people I cared for adequately, nor could I make consistently tolerable decisions and actions because I was always at the mercy of what someone else*

thought I should say or do or I simply did not know what to do if someone didn't tell me. I was always looking outside myself as I had no idea where a self like this even came from let alone how to effect it , to shape it, to manage it, to inform it.

We have seen that Clean Language and Symbolic Modeling maintain all attention within the client's own psychic space, by keeping all interaction "clean" from external influence. The client decides and owns their desired outcome, and they declare when they achieve it. The facilitator is not responsible for interjecting solutions, ideas, or suggestions.

In a Clean context, there is nothing to fix because there is nothing wrong or broken in the system as it is. The client's present experience is what it is. The only reference is the experience they would choose to have.

The client already possesses the resources they need, and they can use thoughts, logic and the process of *self-modeling* (noticing and reflecting on one's own patterns) to come up with new ideas and solutions that mean something particular to them and thereby build the model they mean to effect in their life.

I'll explain what self-modelling is by revisiting the session where I explored my relationship with my mother's communication. You will recall that her words that, to me, were sticky burrs that attached themselves to me, and which I could not escape.

The process of realizing and expressing that connection is modelling. I spoke into reality a metaphor that was true for me. I had the very real sense — the embodied experience — of being unable to shake off those things my mother would say.

Through feeling those feelings, right then in the present moment, I could see how I was functioning when that kind of communication happened. So that's my model. It has nothing to do with the past. There is no "this because that." Past events are past events and are unchangeable. It has every-thing to do with what is going on in my body, right here, right now.

(So, we might go on to ask, does it have anything to do with my mother at all?)

I was then able to attend to the question, "When those words that stick to me and I can't shake off... what would I like to have happen?"

To create a new metaphor is *re-modelling*. It isn't positive thinking, nor affirmation... It started with my realizing that my model was not giving me the outcome I desired. So I changed my model. I could do that because *it was my model*. It wasn't a result of things that happened. It wasn't explained to me by an expert using someone else's ideas. It wasn't my mother's fault. It was just entirely mine. And I had complete control.

My mother didn't change. The past was unaltered. The change was that I put down one model (a tool for making sense of the world and my place in it, which did not serve me), and chose to use one that could help me move toward my desired outcome.

The ability to see our own models in real time, and then to choose, is what we mean by self-modelling. And it is a skill that seems to come naturally to human beings.

Because all information is the client's, they maintain total responsibility for their outcome. The facilitator is primar-ily there to help *slow down the process* and direct attention so that the client can fully engage with their own intrinsic models of the world in the present moment, which is the key to enabling them to create new models that may carry them toward their desired outcome.

Being information-centered, rather than client-centered, the facilitator's attention is not on the client, but actually on the rapport *between the client and the information* that the client has that may be helpful to them. Rapport between client and facilitator is not the primary issue. Our goal is to guide them to relate to the knowledge they already have, and any emergent knowledge that may come forth.

The net effect of maintaining all responsibility with the client within a space free of judgement is actually incredibly empowering for the client. We recognize that the client is fully capable of holding their own pain and suffering in their current system. They were doing it before they came into the therapy room, and I choose to think that this shows what a capable person they already are. They do not come to us because they were incapable, but to find a different way of being.

Maintaining this strict psychic boundary is also liberating for the Clean facilitator, as it removes any need to over-empathize or to take on the client's problems (what is sometimes called *counter-transference*). Not being required to provide solutions allows us to listen with maximum awareness and focus.

The psychologist and priest Anthony De Mello viewed psychology as designed more to make people feel better than to teach the therapist how to sit with *what is* for a client. For De Mello, blending spiritual and therapeutic service meant simply being with the client in a state of respectful patience and total acceptance, giving them the chance to grow within the experience.

Free from Dependency

It should be clear now that Clean Language, if followed correctly, cannot create an environment conducive to client-therapist dependency.

The Clean facilitator does not use their training, intelligence, and effort to deliver solutions. In fact, the client does the work, and constructs their own solution.

To put it another way, we don't provide a model — we are modeling and this in turn leads clients towards a the skill of *self-modeling*.

In the best-case scenario, when a person gets good at modeling, they are able to notice what is going on with them in real time, and then to ask, "When that happens, what would I like to have happen?" They can start to envision a desired future that often clarifies actions that they may need to take.

One thing that happens in clean as a person begins to self model is they gain greater self-sufficiency in a way that allows for greater autonomy as well as the ability to work more closely with others. When someone learns how to self-model, they learn to find ways to their own solutions faster, and eventually can do that without facilitation, ending their need for outside intervention.

The following testimony comes from a client who has experienced Clean Language and Symbolic Modeling after other therapies, who shares how his experience with Clean has helped him not only to own his own identity, but also to respect others' realities in a new way...

> *The difference between Clean and therapy or hypnotherapy is I'm using my imagination more to solve my problems. Talk therapy doesn't add up for me, saying my identity comes from genetics or my upbringing. I'm sure there's truth in that, but maybe it's a made-up model that was put into folklore. So now, I'm much more empowering myself. I know what motivates me. I'm like my own coach now.*
>
> *If I'm not given the ability to build my own identity, my internal reference, through self-modeling and imagination, then I can't build self with any kind of meaning, because the responsibility and the meaning will be given over to someone else, and it could be a*

god, or it could be a therapist, but where does that get me?

Without that, Symbolic Modeling and Clean Language, I could not support the identity that I'm building. What I've learned from Clean is, what's really effective is to let those I'm with have their own reality, and I need to find a way to meet them where they are. If I can't accept the 'factness' of how that is for my friend, how can I do it for me? And where does that leave me?"

Bringing Clean Into Therapy

While Clean Language originally came from a therapeutic background, it is not specifically a therapeutic method, more a methodology. To quote James Lawley, "A process or methodology takes place over time, involving a number of stages/phases which when taken together make up a coherent approach". In my experience, it is extremely flexible, working very well in a therapeutic context as well as in business and in coaching.

I believe its great flexibility is due to the fact that what we are really doing is showing the client *how to model*, and that can be used for whatever the client may wanting. It happens to work at a very deep level, identity level, the level of the client's *being*, rather than just their external *doing*. Clean Language is particularly good at working alongside — or even within — other therapy models, like a lowest common denominator in arithmetic.

I must stress that, despite being apparently incredibly simple and very quick to learn, and not requiring the facilitator to be "clever", it requires a level of mental rigor and discipline unlike anything else I have used.

My metaphor for learning Clean Language is very much like learning the guitar — easiest instrument to learn, hardest to master. Almost anyone can pick up a guitar and learn five or six chords, which will let them play an enormous number of tunes. And yet, the guitar has so much variability in tunings and playing styles that it can take a lifetime to begin to master all the possibilities.

In the same way, it is easy to learn some of the basic Clean Language questions and put them to good use in your work and relationship, using them individually or in small useful models, a bit like chords. And learning the entire methodology of Symbolic Modeling is like learning how to use each string and tune differently for variation of sound and effect, each question with each person being the creation of something new and yet — like music — frequently combining patterns that when followed tend to work well together.

Also, the subtleties that emerge as you practise Clean Language mean that you'll never stop learning. Just working with the complexity within another human being is challenging on its own. The learning is immediate and iterative, each question adding more information and each shift of attention and skill creating its own benefits and challenges.

Personally, I found the intellectual challenge was not diminished in any way when I started using Clean. I'm still an avid reader about new science and theories.

I should also add that this is still such a new discipline that every Clean practitioner today can be counted among the pioneers.

There is also a handy model that we use called *PRO* (Problem, Remedy, Outcome) which is designed to help the facilitator, especially a new practitioner, from getting into a negative mix. If you use this model, you can be confident you'll be doing what's in the client's best interests, and not go off track.

Conclusion

Could Clean Support Your Therapy Work?

Is there a place for therapy in today's world? Absolutely. I would never argue that we should drop the psychological models that have been practised and developed over several generations. As we've seen, talk therapy works. Not every time, but there are circumstances where the right method serves the specific client. However, I think it is very likely that some personalities simply do not get on with talk therapy, for reasons that probably come down to one or more of those six disadvantages.

If you are a therapist, and you find your regular model doesn't work for a particular client, consider whether the cause may derive from one or more of the potential failure points in classic talk therapy. In that situation, you may choose to try Clean techniques.

You might ask your client, "I'm wondering if the methods we've been using are not working for you. Would you be interested in trying something different to what we have been doing?" which is respectful both to the client and the process, and then try Symbolic Modeling, which is naturally free from the disadvantages of classic talk therapy.

If you become skilled in Symbolic Modeling, whether or not you go on to use it as part of your therapy toolset, and regardless of the therapy format you use, you will certainly apply the core skill of *modeling...* for yourself and other aspects of your life.

I would not wish to say that Clean Language or Symbolic Modeling is *the* answer. Any true professional should continually question their theories, models, and methods. If we view our profession from a scientific perspective, we should never claim that its methods are finalized. Science does not claim that something is known to be a fact and will never be disproved . True science can only say, "This theory or practice is what *seems to work today*, and we will continue to be open to improvements and changes as more information becomes available."

We should also continually seek to integrate new knowledge, new science, into our existing models. In particular, recent advances in cognitive linguistics, cognitive science, and self organizing systems theory have a huge amount to offer the practising therapist.

I love to witness the "Aha!" moment that so many people get when they understand how Clean Language works. Many people I work with seem to have a "Clean-shaped hole". They find it fits their integrity, how they want to work with people, and offers them a way to achieve what they've wanted to do — help people in a respectful and unobtrusive way.

I hope this book has given you at least a flavor of what is possible. If you think Clean Language may have something to offer you, perhaps ask yourself the clean question, "What would I like to have happen next?"

What I would like to have happen is to be part of a culture, a global *clean* culture, based on Clean Language. This would be a multidisciplinary community united in its belief in the sovereignty of every individual, where we can freely share our experiences of applying these simple and powerful methods in more and more disciplines.

Imagine a world where relationships ceased to be adversarial, where diversity stopped meaning tolerance and instead became celebration, where each person's view and experience of the world were respected as 'true" for them, where others weren't threatened by difference but excited by it instead. Where questioning became the norm rather than telling and each person was seen as whole and capable regardless of their circumstances.

It will begin with all of us learning how to respect other people, respect their experience of the world unquestioningly, without judgement of whether it's right or wrong or even makes sense.

That's why I started the Clean Language Institute, which is the only certifying Clean Language training available in the United States today [the only clean language training available in the US today that provides an internationally recognized certification as a Clean Facilitator].

If you interested in being one of the early adopters of Clean Language, please visit cleanlanguagetraining.com to find out about our introductory and full training courses, starting with the Client Clarity Summit, which is the ideal introduction to Clean Language.

Acknowledgments

This is a living document and will be updated as an changes or additions are made to the manuscript - either due to the authors updated model and opinion or new evidence that can contribute to the content in a vital way.

This small book has been through the hands of many people during its development; from teachers of Clean Language to those who have been long term therapy clients. The feedback and suggestions have varied and one consistent thread came through...this book has some very good points that are worth thinking about!

I would like to thank Penny Tompkins and James Lawley for their review and feedback. They have been encouraging, gifting me with their time and feedback. Their feedback has given me many good things to think about, references to draw on and ways to make this book better in the future.

James Ramirez has been an unfailing support and encouragement both in my creative ventures and the training rooms of the Clean language Institute. As an advocate for the mentally ill through NAMI, James would love to see Clean be integrated into the therapy room and mental health models.

Ben Hunt, I could not have done it without him. I came to Ben early on to help me with my website, but I have come away with so much more. This book is the result of a series of many interviews over a period of many months.

Lynn Mathews Parks, my design editor and extraordinary friend. Without her unfailing eye for detail and curiosity this print version would not be possible.

And to Irene Neale, Simone Banghard, Lynndal Daniels, Katie Raver, and others in my life that helped me with this endeavor through encouragement, feedback, suggestions and reactions to the material that have been invaluable.

Legal Stuff

This book is designed to provide information and motivation to our readers and is presented solely for educational and entertainment purposes. The content is the sole expression and opinion of its author based on personal observations and years of experience, and not necessarily that of the publisher.

This publication contains ideas, opinions, and information on how you can improve your clients success. The materials are intended to provide helpful and informational material on the subject addressed in the publication. The publisher and author do not provide you with any medical, health, psychological or professional advice or service or any other personal professional service.

The publisher and author, jointly and severally, make no representation or warranties with respect to accuracy, reliability, sufficiency or completeness of the contents of this publication and specifically disclaim any implied warranties or merchantability or fitness for any particular purpose. There are no warranties with extend beyond the descriptions contained in this paragraph. The accuracy and completeness of the information provided herein and the opinions stated are not guarantees nor warranties to or towards the production of any particular result, and the advice, strategies contained herein may not be suitable for every individual.

You read this publication with the explicit understanding that neither the publisher, nor author shall be liable for any direct or indirect loss of profit or any other commercial damages, including but not limited to special, incidental, punitive, consequential or other damages. In reading or using any part or portion of this publication, you agree not to hold, not attempt to hold the publisher or authors liable for any loss, liability, claim, demand, damage and all legal costs or other expenses arising whatsoever in connection with use, misuse or inability to use the materials. In jurisdictions that exclude such limitations, liability is limited to the consideration paid by you for the right to view or use these materials, and/or the greatest extent permitted by law.

Endnotes & Resources

On Symbolic Modeling and Clean Language

Lawley, James & Tompkins, Penny. *Metaphors in Mind: Transformation through Symbolic Modelling*. Developing Company Press, UK, 2000.

Lawley, James & Tompkins, Penny. *DVD: Strong and Strange Sensation*. Developing Company Press, UK, 2004.

Sullivan, Wendy & Reese, Judy. *Clean Language: Revealing Metaphors and Opening Minds*. Crown House Publishing; 1 edition (December 30, 2008)

Campbell, Gina. *Mining Your Metaphors: A How-To Work book on Clean Language and Symbolic Modeling*. BalboaPress (March 3102)

On Basics of Facilitation

Campbell, Gina. *Mining Your Metaphors: A How-To Work book on Clean Language and Symbolic Modeling, Basics Part 2: Facilitating*. BalboaPress, 2013

Harland, Philip. *Trust Me, I'm the Patient: Clean Language, Metaphor, and the New Psychology of Change*. Wayfinder Press, Ridgway, CO. 2012.

Harland, Phillip. *The Power of Six: A Six-Part Guide to Self Knowledge*. Lulu Press, 2009

Way, Marian. *Clean Approaches for Coaches*. Clean Publishing, 2013

Cooper, Lynn & Castellino, Mariette. *The Five Minute Coach: Improve Performance Rapidly*. Crown House Pub Ltd, 2012

Walker, Caitlin. *From Contempt to Curiosity: Creating the Conditions for Groups to Collaborate Using Clean Language and Systemic Modelling.* Clean Publishing, 2014

On Cognitive Linguistics and Science

Lakoff, George & Johnson, Mark. *Metaphors We Live By.* University Of Chicago Press, 1980

Lakoff, George & Turner, Mark. *More than Cool Reason: A Field Guide to Poetic Metaphor.* University Of Chicago Press, 1989

Johnson, Mark. *The Body in the Mind: The Bodily Basis of Meaning, Imagination, and Reason.* University Of Chicago Press, 1990

Bergen, K. Benjamin. *Louder Than Words: The New Science of How the Mind Makes Meaning.* Basic Books, 2012

Turner, Mark. *The Origin of Ideas: Blending, Creativity, and the Human Spark.* Oxford University Press, 2014

Finally, some books on other methods that have a taste of clean intention

Eugene Gendlin. *Focusing.* Bantam Books; 2nd (revised) edition, 1982.

Anne Wilson Schaef. *Beyond Therapy, Beyond Science.* HarperSanFrancisco 1992

Paul Z Jackson and Mark McKergow. *The Solutions Focus - Making Coaching & Change SIMPLE.* (2nd edition) 2006

Robert Dilts & Judith Delozier. *NLP II: The Next Generation.* 2010 (for Generative NLP)

Links & Resources

This book was originally designed as an ebook and most of the resource links were applicable to an online environment. Here are the links in short form for your review or you can visit http://cleanlanguagetraining.com/eotlinks/ for an online collection of the external links referenced below.

Introduction

1. http://tinyurl.com/2auqqzr

2. http://tinyurl.com/khnyfvt

3. http://tinyurl.com/lpqvy24

4. http://tinyurl.com/l2bfmng

5. http://tinyurl.com/mnkpqmk

Why Therapy Isn't Working

6. http://tinyurl.com/250e6de

Is The Client At Fault

7. http://tinyurl.com/490ebwu

Is The Therapist At Fault

8. http://tinyurl.com/ny5wzt2

Is The Method At Fault

9. http://en.wikipedia.org/wiki/Dodo_bird_verdict

Unequal Power Relationship

10. http://www.aa.org/assets/en_US/smf-121_en.pdf

11. http://tinyurl.com/kexauco

Intrusive Methods

12. http://tinyurl.com/490ebwu

Externalizing Responsibility

13. http://www.zurinstitute.com/burnout.html

14. http://psycnet.apa.org/journals/pro/19/6/624/

The Client Is Empowered

15. http://tinyurl.com/mw8r55b

Free From Unequal Power Relationships

16. http://en.wikipedia.org/wiki/Facilitator

Free From Intrusive Methods

17. http://tinyurl.com/llyburv

Notes

Notes

Notes

Notes